Warriors and Wailers

One Hundred Ancient Chinese Jobs You Might Have Relished or Reviled

By Sarah Tsiang
Art by Martha Newbigging

annick press
toronto + new york + vancouver

© 2012 Sarah Tsiang (text)
© 2012 Martha Newbigging (art)
Edited by Barbara Pulling
Designed by Sheryl Shapiro
Additional Image Credits: Chinese zodiac paper cuts (top border), © Ferguswang; blue
mountains (footer graphic), © Makhnach; silhouette of bonsai, © Tatyana Zolotareva;
dragon (chapter graphic), © Katya Triling; bamboo, © Irina Matyash; chapter banners with
cherry blossoms, © Jadehawk: all © Dreamstime.com.

A sincere thank-you to expert reader Lin Fan, Departments of East Asian Studies
and Art History and Communication Studies, McGill University.

Annick Press Ltd.

We acknowledge the support of the Canada Council for the Arts, the Ontario Arts
Council, and the Government of Canada through the Canada Book Fund (CBF) for
our publishing activities.

ONTARIO ARTS COUNCIL
CONSEIL DES ARTS DE L'ONTARIO

Cataloging in Publication

Tsiang, Sarah
    Warriors and wailers : one hundred ancient Chinese jobs you might have relished
or reviled / by Sarah Tsiang ; art by Martha Newbigging.

(Jobs in history)
Includes index.
ISBN 978-1-55451-390-1 (pbk.).—ISBN 978-1-55451-391-8 (bound)

    1. Occupations—China—History—Juvenile literature.
2. China—History—221 B.C.-960 A.D.—Juvenile literature.
I. Newbigging, Martha II. Title. III. Series: Jobs in history series

HD8735.T75 2012   j331.700951   C2011-907158-4

Distributed in Canada by:
Firefly Books Ltd.
66 Leek Crescent
Richmond Hill, ON
L4B 1H1

Published in the U.S.A. by Annick Press (U.S.) Ltd.
Distributed in the U.S.A. by:
Firefly Books (U.S.) Inc.
P.O. Box 1338
Ellicott Station
Buffalo, NY 14205

Printed in China.

Visit us at: www.annickpress.com
Visit Sarah Tsiang at: http://sarahtsiang.wordpress.com
Visit Martha Newbigging at: http://marthanewbigging.com

Note: In Chinese, *qi* is
pronounced *chi.*

For my father, Ming lo (Kenneth) Tsiang (1943–1999), 蔣民陸,
who, had he lived in ancient China, would have been a redresser of wrongs.
—S.T.

To Debbie
—M.N.

CONTENTS

Introduction/6

What Happened When?/8

Rank and Honor/11

Education/13

Women in Imperial China/14

Religion and Schools of Thought/15

Chapter 1. Imperial Jobs/18
Emperor/19, Empress/Empress Dowager/20, Child Emperor, Heir Apparent/21,
Grand Tutor to the Heir Apparent/21, Imperial Consort/22, Sacred and Divine Empress Regnant/23,
Minister of the Household/23, Minister of the Guards/24, Minister Herald/24,
Minister Steward/25, Court Architect/25, Eunuch/26, Pekingese Caretaker/26

Chapter 2. Noble Jobs/27
King/28, Princess/29, Guest/29, Consort Family/30, Concubine/30, Noblewoman/31

Chapter 3. Civil Service Jobs/32
Imperial Chancellor/33, Minister Coachman/33, Grand Administrator/34, County
Administrator/34, Minister of the Imperial Clan/35, Minister of Finance/35, Mail Carrier/36

Chapter 4. Academic Jobs/37
Private Teacher/38, Student/38, Historian/39, Woman Scholar/39, Astronomer/40,
Astrologist/40, Alchemist/41, Geomancer/42, Inventor/42, Philosopher/43

Chapter 5. Religious Jobs/44
Minister of Ceremonies/45, Royal Oracle/Bone Diviner/45,
Priest/46, Sorceress/46, Buddhist Monk or Nun/47,
Shaolin Warrior Monk/48

Chapter 6. Life, Death, and Well-being Jobs/49
Doctor/50, Medical Professor/51, Acupuncturist/51,
Midwife/52, Wet Nurse/53, Physiognomist/53,
Veterinarian/54, Professional Wailer/54, Matchmaker/55

Chapter 7. Law & Order and Military Jobs/56
Magistrate/57, Minister of Justice/58, Prefect/58,
Gold Bird Guard/59, Market Commandant/59,
Military Service—Conscripted/60, Female Warrior/61,
Watchtower Guard, Great Wall/62

Chapter 8. Peasant Jobs/63
Female Peasant/64, Male Peasant/65,
Endless Chain Worker/65,
Night Soil Spreader/66,
Cormorant Fisher/66, Silk Maker/67

Chapter 9. Corvée Labor, Convict Labor, and Slavery Jobs/68
Great Wall Builder/69, Grave Digger/70, Salt Mine Worker/70,
Litter Attendant/71, Dark Green Head/72, Government Slave/72

Chapter 10. Artisans and Performers/73
Opera Actor/74, Acrobat/75, Musician/75, Printer/76, Paper Maker/77, Poet/78, Calligrapher/79,
Ink Stick Maker/80, Painter/80, Bronze Worker/81, Illusionist/81, Pillow Maker/82, Iron
Worker/82, Lacquer Worker/83, Jade Worker/83, Master Craftsman, Terra-cotta Warriors/84

Chapter 11. Merchants and Service Worker Jobs/85
Merchant Junk Sailor/86, Proto Banker/87, Tea Merchant/87,
Noodle Maker/88, Restaurant Worker/88,
Pearl Maker/89, Slave Merchant/89

Chapter 12. Illegal Jobs/90
Pirate Admiral/91, Assassin/91, Rebel Leader/92,
Redresser of Wrongs/92, Fake Buddhist Monk/93,
Robber/Beggar/Vagabond/93

Recommended Further Reading/94

Acknowledgments/94

Index/95

INTRODUCTION

Pirates, magicians, imperial intrigue, and inventions that changed the world: ancient China was an amazing and vibrant place, unique in customs, beliefs, and achievements. With 4,000 years of history and one of the most advanced societies in the world, China has more than its share of wonders. Where would we be without paper, compasses, or printing? The history of the ancient Chinese affects the history of the world.

While Europeans were treating sick people by having barbers slice them open to bleed out the illness, the ancient Chinese were taking pulses and prescribing a healthier diet and more exercise. The confident Chinese didn't think much of the rest of the world in this or other respects. They felt that they were surrounded by "barbarians," and were proud of their very advanced society. Though they received visits from English and Dutch delegations, the Chinese found Europeans less than impressive. But while diplomacy with this part of the world was limited, trade was not. The Chinese established the Silk Road trade network, using it to trade with Romans and Persians. Extending this network throughout Asia, the powerful Chinese navy explored and traded with India, Sri Lanka, Cambodia, and many other countries. And China didn't just consider itself superior to all other nations—it saw itself as their ruler. The Chinese emperor was believed to rule everything under the sun. Since China was considered the "middle kingdom" (the center of civilization), naturally, it was thought, that was where the emperor of all creation concentrated his time and energy.

China is one of the largest countries in the world. It stretches over 5,000 kilometers (3,100 miles) and encompasses both

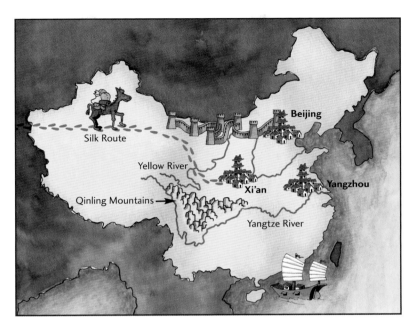

subtropical and subarctic weather. Some regions, like south of the Qinling Mountains, receive summer monsoons, while in the north and west there can be no rain at all throughout the year. The country is home to huge mountain ranges, broad plains, vast deserts, fertile lowlands, and sea coasts.

Though the reigning emperor in ancient China ruled all of this enormous area, kings and grand administrators ruled the various kingdoms and commanderies. Each of those included 10 or 20 prefectures, which were about the size of English counties. The prefectures were further divided into districts that covered small towns and villages.

China had a pretty big population even in, say, the Tang Dynasty (618–907 CE). According to the national census, in the year 742 there were about 50 million people. By comparison, Canada in 2010 had just over 34 million, and the US, just over 308 million people. Though the great majority of people in ancient China were farming peasants, the society of the time included everything from musicians to scholars to diviners.

WHAT HAPPENED WHEN?

Although this book covers a long period of time, most of the jobs you'll read about are described as they would have been performed between the Han Dynasty and the Tang Dynasty.

WHO RULED?

"Dynasty" was the period of time in which one family ruled successively, with the younger generation taking the place of the older generation. The system sounds neat and easy, but usually a dynasty didn't end with a peaceful transition. New dynasties often started before the overthrow of the ruling one. Sometimes different regions were ruled by different groups, and it could take a long time for one winner to come out on top. China was such a big place that it would take years for everyone in the country to learn that the ruling dynasty had changed.

c. 1600–1050 BCE: Shang Dynasty

The Shang Dynasty produced the earliest evidence of a writing system and of historical records. Archeologists have found tens of thousands of inscribed oracle bones from this period, as well as bronze, jade, stone, bone, and ceramic artifacts. The upper class lived in splendor, but most people were farming peasants who hunted to supplement their diet. Ancestor worship was widely practiced.

Taoism, Confucianism, and Buddhism started to gain influence. Though Buddhism was founded in the 5th century BCE in ancient India (the founder living at the same time as Confucius), it took much longer to spread its influence in China. The Zhou Dynasty asserted the idea of the "mandate of heaven." Iron was discovered—a great boon to farmers, who loved their new, sturdier plows.

Growing settlements in China began to clash, and most small city-states were annexed by larger ones, though some formed alliances to avoid getting swallowed up. Large city-states prevailed. The King of Qin gained dominance by conquering major cities.

c. 1050–256 BCE:
Zhou Dynasty

c. 481–256 BCE:
Warring States Period

256–206 BCE:
Qin Dynasty

The standardization of everything from weights and measurements to the size of chariot axles got under way. The army was centralized. When the Qin Dynasty came to power, common people were not allowed to keep books (except on subjects like medicine or tree planting). At the height of Qin Dynasty the emperor tried to purge all traces of other dynasties and schools of thought by burning books and burying scholars alive. When the emperor died in 210 BCE, an entire terra-cotta army (complete with terra-cotta horses and real weapons) was buried with him. Work on the Great Wall of China and several other large government projects began. Heavy taxes were imposed on the peasantry.

Paper was invented. The government took over the production of salt and iron to gain control of the economy. Buddhism arrived in China, as Buddhist monks started to arrive from India along the trade routes. Eunuchs rose in power. As Taoist rebels gained force, the ruling dynasty started to topple.

The Sui seized power in the north of China, and by 589, one emperor ruled all of China. Emperor Wendi created a large civil service selected through the system of Confucian exams. The Grand Canal, along with some other expensive projects and some bad military campaigns, bankrupted the nation. The poor suffered under high taxation and forced labor.

206 BCE–220 CE: Han Dynasty	220–589 CE: Period of Disunity	581–618 CE: Sui Dynasty	618–907 CE: Tang Dynasty

China was divided into several smaller kingdoms. Different families ruled separate regions over a period of 400 years, with many short-lived dynasties ruling in whole or in part before being defeated. The north and south were divided, and the Sui Dynasty ruled the south. Buddhism spread across China, gaining support in both northern and southern governments.

The civil service exams were made even more difficult. A middle class began to form in cities. Paper money appeared. Wu Zhao, the empress, exerted strong influence in the Tang court, especially after the emperor died. She ruled first as regent and then as empress until 705 CE.

RANK AND HONOR

In imperial China, everyone had a particular place, or rank, in society. The emperor was at the very top, followed by nobles, who formed an extremely small and exclusive group. Next came scholars and civil servants, people who had made their way based on their intelligence. The third level of society was composed of peasant farmers. Most people in China were in this category. Farmers were poor, but they were respected for their very important job of providing the nation with food. Below farmers came the artisans and craftspeople, who made everything from simple pots to gorgeous lacquered hair pins. The lowest and least honorable level of society was reserved for merchants. Since merchants didn't grow or make anything, they were considered parasites who lived off the hard work of others. People such as message runners, butchers, and doctors were harder to classify, but everyone knew where he or she stood in society.

Rank and the rules that went with it were extremely important. As a peasant, you could get into huge trouble for even looking at the emperor. By becoming a high-ranking civil servant, you could bring great honor to your family. Merchants were forbidden to dress in certain clothing or to serve more dishes at their table than the government directed.

Everyone, however, even the emperor, could experience a change in rank. Up until the time of the Shang Dynasty, the emperor and his family were believed to be exalted beings whose power came from heaven. But after the Zhou Dynasty defeated the Shang, they had to come up with an explanation for why they should be allowed to rule instead. The answer was the "mandate of heaven," which stated that if an emperor was corrupt or had displeased the gods, the gods would allow a rebel group to rise up and overthrow him. Once a rebel leader became emperor, the deposed emperor and his sons were usually put to death.

EDUCATION

Today, many people strive for the salary and security that go with a government job. But in ancient China, a job in the civil service was the ultimate ideal—it meant you were set for life. If you wanted to make your parents proud, you wouldn't become a doctor. Instead, you would dream of passing the difficult civil service exams and climbing the ladder of government rank.

To pass the imperial exams, you needed an education. In theory, the exams were open to any male candidate in China. In reality, education was only for those who could afford it. While there were some expensive private schools for the sons of nobles and other high-ranking people, most students paid a tutor for their education. That meant you needed both money and enough time to study. Throughout history, there were a few examples of poor farmers who managed to work all day, study all night (sometimes doing extra chores for a tutor instead of paying him), and then pass the exams to achieve a better life. But these peasants were the exception rather than the rule.

ON YOUR OWN MERITS

Your dad might be a merchant, or a farmer, or an official, but that didn't mean you'd end up with the same job or rank. The Chinese had a strong system of meritocracy (finding the best person for the job). Even if you were a pig farmer, you had the chance to rise to the highest levels of society—provided you could find the time to study for the civil service exams. Meritocracy was a philosophy that guided who was chosen for certain government positions. The Chinese were greatly influenced by the famous philosopher Confucius, who promoted the idea of meritocracy.

WOMEN IN IMPERIAL CHINA

Imperial China was not the best place for women who wanted independence or a career outside the home. Women were considered inferior to men and were expected to be submissive. Ban Zhao, a scholar and historian during the Han Dynasty, wrote in her book *Lessons for Women* that women's role was

> "To be modest, yielding, and respectful; to put others first, and herself last … Strength is the glory of men; weakness is women's good quality. Thus in self-cultivation, nothing equals respect for others; in avoiding confrontation with strength, nothing equals compliance. Therefore it is said that the way of respect and compliance is woman's great *li* [proper rule of conduct]."

Women did not have the same rights or powers as men. As wives, they were expected to be subordinate to their husbands and to their in-laws, too. Of course, that wasn't always what happened. Even in imperial China, women managed to distinguish themselves on the battlefield, as rebel leaders, as pirates, or even, in one case, as reigning empress. Quite a few noblewomen became scholars, poets, and historians. In these and many other ways, women left their indelible mark on the history of imperial China.

RELIGION AND SCHOOLS OF THOUGHT

The oldest form of religion in China is ancestor worship. In this religion, honoring your elders does not stop when they die. Practitioners believe that everybody has a continued existence after death. The souls of those who have died still need nourishment, and they can still help or affect the living. People try to provide happiness and well-being to all the family members in the afterlife.

There are also three major schools of thought in China: Confucianism, Taoism, and Buddhism. Unlike in many other religions or philosophies, people don't need to choose one over the other. Many Chinese have blended parts of each, as well as ancestor worship, into their faith practices.

The famous Chinese philosopher Confucius (actually Kong Fuzi) was a wandering scholar. He traveled to persuade rulers with his ideas. Though rulers paid little attention to him, he spent his later life compiling the Confucian classics. He believed that everyone must know his or her proper place in society to find happiness. You needed to obey and respect your superiors as well as be kind and merciful to your inferiors. These ideals for living applied to everything, from family life to the ruling of a kingdom.

Much later, Chinese government was based on Confucian ideals. Confucius, as a scholar, was very big on learning (surprise, surprise), and the government eventually made the memorization of more than 425,000 words from his texts mandatory for anyone taking the civil service exams. Followers of Confucius believed and promoted the ideas of justice, obligation, and order.

Taoism didn't hold with the idea that everything should depend on a strict hierarchy. Instead, Taoists believed that people should turn to nature as an example of how to live correctly. They strove for harmony and looked to a simple life that followed the rhythms of the natural world. They believed this would bring people closer to the *Tao*, the source of life and order in the universe.

Buddhism originated in ancient India. An Indian prince, one of many Buddhas, taught that unhappiness was caused by desire. He offered an eightfold noble path: right understanding, right thought, right speech, right action, right livelihood, right moral effort, right mindfulness, and right concentration. If people managed to do all eight *at the same time*, they could achieve enlightenment and endless bliss.

Blending all three philosophies is so common in China that there is even a name for it: "the three ways that flow into one."

China was a land of firsts: the Chinese invented the magnetic compass, gun powder, porcelain, the bristle toothbrush, silk, cast iron, the crossbow, and toilet paper (to name just a few of the things we take for granted today). Imperial China had enough stories of intrigue, scandal, rebellion, and triumph to fill a library. It would take you your whole life to read *everything* on the history and daily life of the ancient Chinese. This book will take only a few hours. It's a small sampling of the different jobs that you might have loved or hated had you lived in imperial China.

Imperial Jobs

The imperial palace was like a small, exclusive city filled with the most glorious luxuries you could imagine. The actual palace, along with its location, changed to suit the dynasty in power, but they all had one thing in common: they were spectacular. Depending on a person's rank, he would either be enjoying these luxuries or providing them for others. A huge range of people worked to serve the emperor, his family, and his court. Everyone from the highest-ranked civil servant to the lowliest slave had a clearly defined job to do, and it was a huge amount of work to keep the palace running smoothly. In fact, emperors often had at least two residences: one for winter and one for summer. In the Tang Dynasty the emperor had a hall cooled by what was probably the first system of air conditioning. Water-powered fan wheels wafted refreshing breezes around the hall, and water was pumped to all four corners, wetting curtains and splashing on the stone floor. Ice was placed under chairs as well. The room could get cold enough on a hot summer day to give people the chills.

Emperor

You have the most powerful boss imaginable—the gods. As one of the "sons of heaven," you enjoy heavenly approval as the sole and supreme ruler of the entire civilized world. Most emperors come from a long line, or dynasty, of fathers and sons. But no one family has the eternal right to rule. It's possible to lose the mandate of heaven by ruling poorly. A natural disaster paired with a successful overthrow will let you know that your time is up. To rule is a divine gift, and it comes with absolute authority as well as awesome responsibility. You have the final word on everything, and you can choose to take a life or start a war with the wave of your hand. You can order someone who displeases you to commit suicide. You can order the wholesale release of slaves. You've done all of these things, and you expect your words to be taken as sacred commands.

Much of your time, though, is spent presiding over lengthy court ceremonies and religious rituals. As the "son of heaven," you are in a unique position to appeal to or appease the gods and ancestors. You are surrounded by hundreds of guards, servants, advisors, concubines, and entertainers (to name a few groups), and yet you're exceptionally alone. Almost nobody is allowed to view your private quarters, and not even your mother is permitted to call you by your given name. No one else on earth has your status, and so there's no one you can relate to as an equal.

Empress/Empress Dowager

You are the emperor's official wife, and any sons you bear will be first in line to the throne. You are not, however, the only woman in your husband's life. The emperor can have thousands of concubines. Concubines are like unofficial wives. They don't have the same status and privileges as the empress, but they hold rank and power in their own right. As long as you have a son, you'll become the empress dowager (mother of the next emperor) and hold the most power when your husband dies. If you don't have a son, though, a concubine could replace you as empress dowager when her son becomes heir.

As empress dowager your status is more or less comparable to that of the emperor, your son. You have great influence over him. If he comes to power while he is still young, you'll be the one to rule all of China. You're supposed to give up your power when your son is old enough to rule, but that doesn't always happen. Empress Dowager Teng in the Han Dynasty ruled until her death, even though the heir was 27 by then. Empress dowager is one of the most powerful positions imaginable. No wonder you want to have a baby boy.

Your future, my precious son, is also mine.

Child Emperor, Heir Apparent

You were born for this job. No, really. As the eldest son of the emperor, you're likely to become the head guy. When your dad dies, you'll become the emperor (even if you're still a baby). If you're too young to assume power, your mom will take charge, and you'll just have to wear a lot of formal clothes and sit through long ceremonies with your hands folded in your lap. Things can get tricky, though. Even after you're officially emperor, your mom may not want to give up her power. Young heirs apparent who appear too eager also have a funny way of getting themselves murdered. I'd keep my dreams of being emperor one day quiet if I were you.

Grand Tutor to the Heir Apparent

Your status as grand tutor to the emperor's heir is highest among all officials. You're also considered a supreme lord. You're supposed to be the moral guide for your young charge, and you're *supposed* to have a lot of power. In reality, though, you're mainly a figurehead. When the heir is underage, it's the empress dowager who makes all the decisions. You just go with the flow. In fact, most grand tutors don't assume the position until they're really, really old. That makes you wonder if maybe the royal family hired you because you're likely to die off soon. Oh well, at least the pay is great and the work minimal. No parent–teacher meetings or report cards to fill out, either.

Imperial Consort

You are one of the emperor's many concubines (he has up to 40,000). You live in your own lavish apartment and have been ranked among all the others, so your official title could be "madame," or "decent lady," or "average talented lady." Maybe one day you'll be "talented lady." Depending on your ranking, your status could be equivalent to a lesser official or as powerful as a king.

Because there are so many of you, there's a chance you'll never even get to see the emperor. That doesn't mean you'll be bored, though. There's enough in-fighting and political drama to last several lifetimes. If the empress doesn't give birth to a son, then your son could be next in line to the throne. There are always rumors of empresses and concubines poisoning each other's sons or plotting an overthrow. Do it with a smile, though, since jealousy is outlawed.

Keeping yourself attractive will give you the best chance of wooing the emperor. So rub bat brains on your skin to get rid of blackheads, and smear your face and body with cream made from the blood of a black-boned, silky bird on the seventh day of the seventh moon. You'll also want to pluck out your eyebrows and paint in new ones, as well as add beauty marks (red, yellow, or black) in the shapes of moons, birds, flowers, or insects.

Between keeping yourself beautiful, making political alliances, and trying to protect your son from being murdered, you lead a busy life.

Sacred and Divine Empress Regnant

This job is very hard to get. In fact, only one person, Wu Zetian, has ever attained the status of empress regnant. She started out as a concubine of the old emperor. When he died, the wife of the new emperor thought Wu Zetian might be useful to keep around. Too bad for her; Wu Zetian beat out the other wife in influence and became the new empress.

Like Wu Zetian, you start your career as empress dowager, but eventually your son yields to your power, and you become the reigning empress in your own right. You work to elevate the status of all women (you're a feminist before there was a word for it), and you favor Buddhism over Taoism because it's less sexist. You're a good leader, lowering taxes for the hard-working peasants and bringing more and more scholars into court. When your son eventually takes over, you'll die with the title of empress.

Minister of the Household

Not only watch the emperor's back, protect the sky above his head and the ground beneath his feet.

There are so many people, jobs, and tasks in the imperial palace that the emperor needs someone important, like you, to oversee everything. Your main job, however, is to make sure your master is safe, both on the palace grounds and whenever he makes an excursion to the outside world in his chariot. As minister of the household, you command five armed cadet corps made up of both soldiers and civilians. Although the emperor trusts you, he doesn't want you to have complete power over his safety, so you're not in charge of those who guard the palace entrances, the emperor's own private apartment, or the residences of the concubines (the whole group was known as the harem). While your job has a lot of perks, hanging out with the beautiful wives of the emperor isn't one of them.

Minister of the Guards

Minister Herald

The imperial palace is completely surrounded by walls, and you're in charge of them. More specifically, you're in charge of making sure that no one gets in who isn't supposed to. Of course, you're too high up in rank to do any actual guarding yourself. That job falls to your prefects, who are stationed along the walls, towers, and gates of the imperial palace. As minister of the guards, you also supervise the complicated system of wood and metal passports issued to keep track of who is on palace grounds. In the event of an attack, the imperial palace is locked down, and all the passports are collected.

Are you a people person? Good at mingling? Then as the palace's director of guests (another of your titles), you'll be in your element. Your job is to properly receive honored guests at court. Guests could be nobles or foreign ambassadors. Those who serve under you will make sure that the guests have elegant living quarters and anything else they require. You'll make sure that the guests *kowtow* properly when presented to the emperor, acknowledging him as the ruler of everything under the sun, including foreign kingdoms. *Kowtowing* means that people must kneel from a standing position three times, and while they are kneeling must touch their foreheads to the ground three times. Stubborn Western diplomats who refuse to kowtow to the emperor won't be allowed an audience. You and your staff are also in charge of seating or placing everyone where they should be during imperial ceremonies and sacrifices.

Minister Steward

Court Architect

You are the go-to guy when the emperor wants things done. New singing girl? No problem. A golden robe made of the finest silk? Coming right up! As the minister steward, you are also in charge of the emperor's money, and you serve him as kind of a personal aide. A large number of people report to you, including the prefect grand physician (the emperor's personal doctor), the court provisioner (he's in charge of the kitchen, the chefs, and all the royal foods), the women who weave for the emperor, and those who tend the palace grounds. You even oversee the bureau of music, which arranges for music at imperial ceremonies and gathers folk songs from throughout the empire for the emperor's pleasure. You have the job of managing the emperor's sizable harem, too. You make sure that the imperial concubines are kept in style. Your office provides for all they need, right down to the ration of 30 liters (27 quarts) of eyebrow pigment.

My design demands perfect symmetry.

Yes, Emperor, right away, Sir.

Verify that order on the double!

You are responsible for most of the construction in the capital city, and much of the maintenance, too. There are so many things that require up-keep: halls, temples, graves, roads, and flood-control works. Most buildings are made of wood, with roofs of ceramic tiles, so there is always the threat of rot or crumbling. You're not going to be out there yourself hammering nails or gathering wood for repairs, but you manage a large staff of laborers who do your bidding. Sometimes it takes up to 100,000 workers to get all the jobs done. It's a good thing you are well paid—even with such a sizable staff, you're still run off your feet.

Eunuch

This job requires two things. First, that you be male. Second, that you be castrated—which means that your testicles have been surgically removed. Eunuchs normally get employment in the palace and an education, and a few lucky ones rise to positions of power and riches. Most eunuchs come from peasant families, and some fathers castrate their own sons to give them the chance at a better life. Being a eunuch is one of the few good jobs that doesn't require a lot of investment, education, or training.

There is a wide range of ranks and jobs for eunuchs, from lowly domestic chores to the emperor's right-hand man. High-ranking eunuchs are often rich, and sometimes even ennobled as marquises. They have their own palaces, often get married, keep concubines, and adopt sons to maintain the family name.

Whole families prosper and are protected if a family member becomes a high-ranking eunuch. Some eunuchs have been elevated to positions of power directly over army generals. If you're a high-ranking eunuch, you will constantly be offered bribes and side deals. You're sure to be embroiled in court intrigues and plots to seize power. Too bad this job comes with such a high entrance fee.

Pekingese Caretaker

You are the eunuch caretaker for the little dogs of the palace. Buddhist monks have selectively bred the Pekingese so it will look like a little lion. Emperors and empresses like having these lion dogs around to help their image. No one else is allowed to possess a Pekingese. If a commoner steals one of these dogs, he or she will be put to death immediately.

The dogs you look after have their own silken apartments. You take them for walks around the imperial gardens, sprinkle them with perfumes, and plump up their beds of bright silk cushions. You also breed the dogs, helping them produce a handsome litter by decorating the chambers of pregnant females with pictures of beautiful puppies, and feeding them only the choicest meats.

The dogs spend long hours at court, sitting near the feet of the emperor. When the emperor walks around, they hold the tail of his robes in their mouths and give precise, sharp barks to announce his arrival. You would protect these dogs with your life.

Chapter 2

Noble Jobs

China was split up into kingdoms ruled by kings and commanderies run by grand administrators (civil servants). Kingdoms were awarded, and to be a king you had to be related to the emperor, usually as an imperial prince. (In earlier times people could be ennobled to the position of king, but then the emperor changed his mind.) Nobles came from three groups: relatives of the emperor, relatives of the empress, and meritorious officials (highly placed officials who were rewarded for doing a really great job). Usually, the relatives of the empress were not only ennobled but given high-ranking civil service jobs. Being or becoming a noble brought with it wealth, prestige, and power.

King

You're family to the emperor: a son, younger brother, or nephew, or a successful general who helped the emperor ascend to the throne. You're supposed to be able to pass down your kingdom to your own son, but it doesn't always happen this way. The emperor might "suggest" that you appoint someone else. Regardless, you live in a huge mansion with tons of servants. You hang out with only the finest society. You probably have quite a few concubines, too, though you're not allowed to have as many as the emperor. You spend your work time in the administration of your kingdom, taking care of the important business that lower officials can't deal with. There are only about 20 kings in all of China, so you rank above just about everyone else.

THE SPORT OF KINGS

Being a king isn't all work and no play. You and your noble friends love to go hunting! You can ride your own horse or take a chariot for the hunt. You love polo so much that you encourage even the palace ladies to have a try at it. You've got dogs (and you sometimes train cheetahs) to chase down prey. When it's time to make the kill, you can show off your archery skills or even use a spear. If you're partial to birds, you might have some falcons, trained birds of prey who will hunt at your command.

Not a fan of hunting? How about a nice game of cards instead? Or a fun bit of gambling? You probably love *liu bo*, a betting game where bamboo sticks are thrown like dice. You also love strategy games like *weiqi* (also known as *go* in Japan) and other board games like Chinese chess. Games are one of the few things that nobles and peasants have in common. Peasants can't afford to have cheetahs hunt for them, but they do gamble and play games in the few free moments they have.

Princess

Guest

Your status is equal to that of a king or a marquis, and you have your own fiefdom and income. You are also the only class of woman who retains her own status after marriage. All other women assume their new husband's status, whether it raises or lowers their position in society. You don't get to choose who you'll marry, however. Your father, the king or emperor, will make that decision, and he'll be looking for the marriage that brings your family the most riches and power. You'll have to leave your family to set up your own household, sometimes in a faraway land. Some princesses have become famous for the beautiful, mournful poetry they wrote after being forced to marry a stranger and move away from everyone and everything they knew. Things aren't all bad, though. You have money and connections, and that will help things between you and your husband. You'll continue to be surrounded by servants and vast wealth, which you can use to exert your influence as well.

It's fun to have rich friends. If you manage to become the guest, or *shike*, of a prince or a very wealthy nobleman, your host will provide lodging, food, clothing, and transportation. If your host really likes you, you may be showered with expensive gifts, like shoes decorated with pearls or a fancy scabbard made from jade and pearls.

Some wealthy hosts have up to 3,000 guests at one time. Some invite only scholars and other prestigious guests. Other hosts want the bragging rights that come with a large number of guests and so they sometimes welcome even fugitives and thieves.

As a guest, you don't have chores to do, but your host may ask you for a favor based on your abilities. If you're an accountant, for example, he might want you to collect his tax. But if your host goes to war you'll be expected to fight and even die for him.

In every other matter you're free to come and go as you please. You expect to be treated politely, and you won't stay on if you don't approve of your host's behavior.

Consort Family

Concubine

Looking good, Sis!

It's not what you know, but who. More importantly, it's who you're related to. It seems your pesky little sister, the one your parents worried would be more of a burden than a help, has caught the emperor's eye, and now your family is moving up in the world. Some families have experienced a huge leap in status when a daughter has become a consort. Empress Dou's family was so poor before she married the emperor that one of her brothers was a slave who made charcoal for his owner. Afterward, they became rich and prestigious. Because of your sister, your family will have access to cushy jobs, wealth, and political power. So be nice to her.

The higher ranked and the richer your husband is, the more concubines he's likely to have— a king or a marquis would likely have 30 to 40. Your position is under the first wife, and you need to wait on her and act humbly. You probably come from a poor family, or maybe you were sold as a slave during a time of famine. But sometimes even higher-born women become concubines. Laws are sometimes passed to allow someone who became a concubine as a result of famine or kidnapping to leave. You are likely skilled as a singer and a dancer. Depending on the time in which you live, you might even have a tutor or some free time available for reading and art. Your main job, though, is to provide a son for the head of the household. The sons of the first wife are considered more legitimate, but if something happens to them, your sons will have a chance at the family fortune and positions. Babies often die in infancy, and powerful men can never have too many sons to ensure the continuation of their family line.

Noblewoman

As the wife of a marquis or a high official, you live a life filled with luxury. You likely have a home in the country as well as one in the city. Both are graced with courtyards and gardens surrounded by walls so that only the best kinds of people can get in. You and your family ride around in an elegant horse-pulled carriage. Tenant farmers work your land for you. You dress in silk gowns and pearls. You like to hold dinner parties at which you serve dishes made from fish, pheasant, quail, turtle, or pork. When you want to get really fancy, you offer your guests delicacies like tiger meat or bear's paw. Of course, you won't be doing the cooking. Your work is of a more refined variety. You spend hours doing delicate embroidery on silk, producing images as complex and lovely as paintings. Embroidery is a good way to express yourself, too; many poems by noblewomen have been found in their needlework. If you live during the Tang Dynasty, you might also spend some time reading and studying. Though it's not often mentioned publicly, many husbands value the well-informed views of their wives.

Chapter 3

Civil Service Jobs

Are you smart? Really, really smart? If so, the civil service might have been for you. It was the most honored profession in ancient China, and you would have gotten tons of perks. The higher you were in the civil service, the better it got. High rank meant riches and special benefits. You might have been the only one allowed to wear a certain color or headdress. (No showing up at a party to discover someone else wearing the same thing.) You were even allowed a special number of courses to be served at your table, in accordance with sumptuary laws.

How did you get this great job? You didn't have to be high status, but you did need to be a boy. You needed years of studying classic texts on history, government, and morality, and then you spent a week in a tiny, prison-like cell writing your final exam. You had to be well prepared because you would be writing out long answers to essay questions. Your penmanship had to be up to snuff because cross-outs or corrections were not allowed. You wouldn't have even thought of cheating. If you were caught cheating, you'd be disqualified, and the examiner, poor guy, would lose his head.

Very few students passed the civil service exams. If you barely passed you might have become a lower official. If you were political, well connected, and a star on your exams, you could rise to the highest heights. So, what are you waiting for? Hit the books!

Imperial Chancellor

I want the latest financial statements, along with the military report and an updated map of the outlying provinces, immediately!

You are as high up as an official can get. Your status is really without parallel. When you visit the emperor, the emperor has to stand up for *you*. If you get sick, the emperor will visit you. The special treatment doesn't end there, either. Normally in Chinese society, you must show your older brother great respect, but your job is so important that you can seat your brother in a less honorable position than your own, and he can't say a word about it.

You have a right to all these benefits because your job is demanding. You look after state finances, the budget, lawsuits, mapmaking, and logistics for military campaigns. You appoint lesser officials and also recommend high-ranking nominees for senior roles. People want to stay on your good side since you're allowed to punish officials without having to go through the emperor first. Money, power, and the ability to lord it over your older brother. What more could you want?

Minister Coachman

Are you looking for a job that has prestige and lets you spend time in the great outdoors? As minister coachman, you supervise the stables, carriages, and coach houses of the imperial palace. More importantly, you provide horses for China's vast army. This is no small task. You need to keep an eye on the huge breeding grounds and the pastures that house the empire's 300,000 war horses. You're boss to tens of thousands of slaves who do the grunt work—feeding, cleaning, and training. Shoveling the poop of 300,000 horses would be too much for any one man. Don't worry, though, you'll still get the glory.

Grand Administrator

County Administrator

You are a very high-ranking civil servant who has been appointed to run one of the commanderies. Rather than inheriting your position, you've worked your way up to commanding this sizable chunk of China. You won't ever be the grand administrator of your home town, though—there's a law against that. You have several commandants who work under you, and they handle the military affairs in your prefectures, like getting conscripts, raising local militias, suppressing bandits, and building beacon towers. But remember—you need permission from the emperor before doing anything beyond your own borders.

Your job is to make sure everything in your commandery is working smoothly. You assign people to check on how well the crops are growing and whether the law is being fairly applied. You need to get acquainted with the families in your commandery because every year you nominate young men for possible positions in the civil service. You have many responsibilities, but yours is a well-paid position that commands a lot of respect.

You take care of a county and report to the grand administrator. There are more than 1,000 counties in ancient China (in 2 CE, there were 1,587 of them), and you work in your county, acting as judge for the county court, police chief, public school administrator, supervisor of public works, census director, head of tax collection, and conscription officer for forced labor. Are you tired yet? All this work, and you get paid for only one job. (Your salary is less than half of that snooty grand administrator's, too.) Luckily, some of your jobs overlap with those of other people, so you don't have to do everything at once. The county magistrate is usually the judge, for example; only if you put someone under arrest will you preside at the trial. Thank goodness for the local elders and village leaders. They handle day-to-day operations, like settling disputes, collecting taxes, and even fighting crime. Seniors are great to have around.

Have you assembled the new conscripts?

The most able and eager in the entire county, Sir!

Minister of the Imperial Clan

Your blood is as blue as it comes. People can rise from other backgrounds to some high-level jobs, but for yours you must have the right breeding and be a member of the imperial family. You're the family's fixer, the person who makes sure everyone is doing what he or she should. You grant things like fiefs (lands) and titles. You maintain the imperial family tree, but the job is more complicated than everyday scrapbooking. You keep a record of all the nobles in China and update it every year.

If another member of the imperial family gets into trouble with the law, you hear about it even before the emperor does. The emperor makes the final decision about what's going to happen to this naughty relative, though. You have no authority over the princes of the family, but the imperial princesses and their fiefs fall under your watchful eye. (Talk about sexist!)

Minister of Finance

Since almost everyone in ancient China is a farmer—though not anyone you socialize with—being the minister of finance is much like being the minister of agriculture. In fact, you could go by either title. You are the tax man, and you collect both cash and crops to take back to the emperor. When the country's yearly budget is calculated, everybody looks to you to come up with the funds. You have the power to set price controls for important commodities, like salt and iron. Since you have to be so precise in your tallies, you're also in charge of setting the standards for units of measurement.

Mail Carrier

Neither snow, nor rain, nor heat, nor gloom of night will keep you from your appointed rounds. Mainly, that's because if the mail is a day late, you'll get 80 blows with a thick rod. You're not really a civil servant, since you didn't pass an exam for your job, but you do work for the government. You're part of a rapid relay system with 1,297 stations (that's one every 16 kilometers [10 miles] along the public roads) that keep horses and donkeys ready to carry orders from the capital and messages from the provinces. You don't want to tire out your animal, so you get a fresh one at each station. The mail is serious business—80 blows is the least penalty you get for being late. The later you are, the worse the punishment, from one year of penal servitude to exile more than 1,071 kilometers (666 miles) from your home district. You can be punished for delivering to the wrong address, for taking the wrong route, or for using a horse if a donkey would have been fast enough. If you're carrying a military message, you'd better whip your horse and ride like the wind because if a battle or the life of a single person is lost due to delayed mail, you'll be sentenced to death by strangulation.

Chapter 4

Academic Jobs

Education was very important. You've heard your mom and dad say it, and if you lived in imperial China, you would have heard everyone else say it, too. Scholars were highly respected, and the best way to get ahead was to study, study, study. For some people, that was easier said than done. Most peasant children, even if they desperately wanted to study, would never have had the opportunity to do so. Being the son of a noble or a rich merchant gave you a much better chance. If your father was a merchant, there was an extra bonus for passing the exams—you could redeem your family's name and put the shame of being merchants behind you.

Private Teacher

While there have been some public schools since the Han Dynasty, private schools flourished after the Song Dynasty. You might be a self-taught scholar, or have attended the school sponsored by your commandery's government, or be a graduate of the impressive imperial academy. If you set up a school in a village or town, the townspeople may build a schoolhouse for you. If you're very popular you could have anywhere from several hundred to more than 1,000 students and they all need to pay for their education. Poor students might pay by collecting firewood or doing tasks you request.

You teach your pupils the basics in literature, philosophy, and mathematics. You guide them onto a righteous path using the teachings of Confucius and other great thinkers. You have them memorize codes of behavior for social and political occasions.

Your students will also sweat over complicated math problems like these: A man is hired as a salt porter. If he is paid 40 *cash* for carrying two measures of salt for a distance of 100 *li*, how much will he be paid for carrying 1.73 measures for a distance of 80 *li*? (The answer, which you know of course, is $27\frac{11}{15}$ *cash*).

Student

You've made it to the imperial university! Forget the apple; you need to present your teacher with silk, jerky, and ale on your first day at school. The state provides you with grain to eat and a place to live. There's quite an age range at your school; boys and young men from 14 to 25 can be admitted. You might get in because your dad has a high rank, or you might be smart enough to have passed a special test.

You'd better be good at memorizing, because you're tested every 10 days. Your master will give you a random sentence from a text, ordering you to recite the 1,000 words that follow. You'll choose a major: law, mathematics, calligraphy, astronomy, calendrical science, divination, or regulations. At the end of the year, you'll sit your final exams. If you fail three years in a row, you'll get sent home without a diploma.

You can skip most of this if you're a child prodigy. During the Tang Dynasty, there was a special test for smart kids nine years old and younger. If you could recite Confucius's *Classic of Filial Piety* and the *Discourses of Confucius* from memory, and correctly answer 10 out of 10 questions on these texts, then you'd be assigned a bureaucratic rank.

This week, only memorize 900 words.

Historian

Woman Scholar

Historians in imperial China were anything but stuffy. When they wrote about historical events, they made the stories exciting, adding dialogue, characters, high adventure, and intrigue. You take your job seriously, but unfortunately, so does the emperor. You'd better make sure he comes across as a really great guy in your book. Poor Sima Qian, who wrote *Records of the Grand Historian*, was sentenced to castration in part because the emperor didn't like his version of events. Sima Qian finished his book nonetheless. He deposited it in the imperial archives and wrote the following words: "If it may be handed down to men who will appreciate it, and penetrate to the villages and great cities, then though I should suffer a thousand mutilations, what regret would I have?" If the emperor likes what you have to say, on the other hand, he might appoint you as court historian. In your work, you're always walking that fine line. Let's hope your version of history only requires of you the sweat and tears of effort, and doesn't cost you other bits of yourself.

Only boys are allowed to study for the civil service exams, so that's not an option for you. The amount of education available to women in ancient China varied from dynasty to dynasty, but even in unenlightened times there were still women scholars. You're probably the daughter of a scholar and grew up helping your dad. When he or your brother dies or is incapable of doing his work, you'll step in to give his lectures or finish the books he was working on. You'll never be given a formal job as a teacher, though you're likely smarter than most of the teachers out there. But you could be in charge of teaching the empress and the imperial concubines. Under some dynasties, women also became famous poets, writers, and thinkers.

Astronomer

Astrologist

You're a scientist working in the most important field of the day. You have a long and proud tradition to draw on. Generations before you have spent time gazing at the stars and recording everything they see. No one would know what year or month it was if it weren't for you. China works on the lunisolar calendar, and it takes a lot of calculation to figure out the important dates, like the New Year, each year.

You also make star maps—charting out the sky and methodically writing and labeling each star. One ancient map documented 1,350 of them! But your observations aren't limited to the stars. You and your colleagues have amazingly complete and accurate records of comets, meteors, supernova stars, and sunspots. You engage in lively debates with your fellow astronomers. Are heavenly bodies round or flat? Is the moon's light a reflection of the sun's light? Your intelligence and your remarkable observations will be a boon to science everywhere. You also work in partnership with another important discipline—astrology.

You are as well respected as an astronomer. In fact, you work very closely with astronomers—their observations of the stars help to inform your predictions. Even the emperor listens closely to your counsel. Your predictions are based on a 60-year cycle that revolves around two other cycles: the five elements (wood, fire, earth, metal, and water) and the twelve animal zodiac signs. The balance of yin and yang and the amount of each of the five elements in a person's makeup will determine his or her personality and future. As an astrologist, you take into account everything that might affect the outcome of both personal and worldly events. You must be well read and well educated for this job.

Jupiter is rising...

...creating an imbalance.

...into the fire cycle...

A very bad sign.

Gulp!

Alchemist

Have you ever wished you could turn your broccoli into chocolate? Alchemists understand. They are on a quest not only to turn lead into gold, but to find the elixir of life. As an alchemist, you work around the clock in a laboratory on a sacred mountain, experimenting with formulas that might make humans immortal. You try all sorts of exotic ingredients, but you're pretty sure that cinnabar (a red mineral) will be part of the winning recipe. After all, you can roast it until it turns into quicksilver—mercury. The emperor would really like to live forever, but watch out. If your latest potion contains a lethal ingredient like arsenic, you might end up killing him instead—a fatal career move for you. Instead, you often test the potions on yourself. Many alchemists have died drinking their own eternal-life potions.

YIN AND YANG

Everything in the world is made of both yin and yang, two natural forces. Yin is dark, cool, damp, and submissive. Yang is bright, warm, dry, and dominant. These forces aren't good or evil, but when they are out of balance, it's bad news. Some objects are more closely associated with one or the other, but there is nothing that is wholly yin or yang, and these forces can ebb or flow over time. The Taijitu symbol (a circle containing both black and white) symbolizes how yin and yang interact and, ideally, balance one another.

Geomancer

Inventor

Your job falls somewhere between those of astrologist and urban planner. Before anyone digs out a burial site or plans a building, you step in with your compass to check that the energy, or *qi*, of the place is right, and that whatever is built will be in harmony with the land. Sometimes you're called in to determine the most auspicious time for an event as well. Your compass is magnetic, and it will form the root of navigation in centuries to come. It has concentric tables that expand out from the middle and provide information on a wide range of data, like time, direction, the elements, astrology, and forms of landscape: everything you need to decide on the best position for an entire city or a single grave site.

Build right here!

You and your peers come from different backgrounds, but you're likely an educated person, and you most likely hold down a good day job. Your peers have invented things like paper, the magnetic compass, printing, and gunpowder. You might be like Zhang Heng, who invented the world's first seismograph (earthquake detector) in 132 CE. This device would alert the emperor when an earthquake happened far away from the imperial palace so that he could quickly send aid to the affected area. It was a jar ringed by eight dragon heads. Each dragon held a small metal ball in its mouth, and under each head was a metal toad with its mouth open. When a distant earthquake sent out tremors undetectable to humans, the pendulum inside the jar swung and knocked a ball out of one of the dragons' mouths into a toad's mouth. The dragon whose ball fell was facing in the direction of the earthquake. This seismograph was so effective that soon after Zhang Heng set up the device, it sensed an earthquake more than 480 kilometers (300 miles) west of the capital. Who knows what your invention will be?

Philosopher

What is the meaning of human existence?

You live in China's golden age of philosophy, from 770 to 221 BCE. You don't hang out with the Greeks, but you would have had a lot in common: the first Greek philosophers puzzled over the same issues at the same time you do. You are an intellectual who travels from place to place, and your services are in high demand. There's no single emperor during your lifetime, but instead a whole bunch of warring regional lords with their own armies. They want you to advise them on the most effective methods of diplomacy, war, and government.

You run a small private school, but you have a lot of competition. There are so many philosophers and schools of thought that your era is known for "the hundred schools of thought." The schools that will eventually come out on top are Confucianism, Taoism, and Buddhism. Right now, though, Mohism and Legalism lead the pack. Mohism calls for universal love for all humans and promotes frugality, pacifism, and divine-rule monarchy. The Legalist school wants to increase the power of the state and build a strong military maintaining the state order through strict law and punishment.

Pacifism or military might? Harmony or right living? What are you going to teach at your school?

Chapter 5

Religious Jobs

In early modern Europe, there were bloody battles over what *every-one* should believe. In imperial China, people treated religious belief a bit like a buffet—they dished up a little Confucianism, a little Taoism, and a little Buddhism, taking the best parts of each to learn about morality and correct behavior. Depending on the dynasty they lived under, and the subjects they chose, students might have memorized passages from Confucian texts or learned about the balance Taoism promoted. During the Tang Dynasty, the reigning empress wanted people to take Buddhism more seriously, and under her rule, monasteries flourished.

Most people conducted ancestor worship as well. Family lines were passed down through father–son relationships, so if a man didn't have a son, he would have no one to attend to him when he died. Everyone knew that when people died, their souls still needed food and drink, as well as money, to help them out in the afterlife. So sacrifices of food, drink, and fake money were offered at the family shrine or temple. Everyone in the family played a role in the sacrifice. Women's duties included preparing the wine and food to be offered. At least spirits usually weren't fussy eaters.

Just about everyone, from the lowliest merchant to the emperor himself, tried in some way to placate the spirits.

Minister of Ceremonies

Royal Oracle/ Bone Diviner

You are the chief official in charge of religious rites, rituals, prayers, and the maintenance of ancestral altars and temples. The emperor depends on you to link him to the supernatural world and to heaven. You have a large staff and a lot of responsibility. One of your subordinates is the court astronomer, who administers the literacy test for those hoping to move up in official circles. The test is no joke—it's composed of 9,000 characters, so you can imagine how well-read your staff is.

The emperor relies on you to answer questions about everything from whether he should go to war to whether his toothache is caused by an angry ancestor. To answer him, you need a piece of bone (usually from an ox) or a turtle shell. First you remove the meat, then you clean the bone or shell carefully, making sure you leave a surface large and smooth enough to write on (these bones are actually the earliest existing scripts). You also drill a small hole, or series of holes, in the bone or shell. Once it's ready, you write out the date and your name. Then, most importantly, you write out your question. During the divination ceremony, you put an intense heat source into the hollows you created, which causes the bone to crack. These cracks hold the answers you're looking for, and you, the diviner, must interpret them. Does that crack look like a yes or a no to you? Thousands of oracle's bones have been discovered in China, so the diviners must have been kept busy.

Priest

Sorceress

The emperor is appointed by heaven and acts on heaven's behalf, so it's natural that the government should also have a hand in the day-to-day religious activities of the people. As a priest, you live in a village, where you're responsible for prayer and the upkeep of your shrine. You prescribe the rites that must be performed to honor the local spirits. The spirits must be carefully attended to. You don't want the lord of the soil or the lord of the crops getting angry and drying everything up.

To worship the spirit of the soil, you create a mound or an altar to mark the spot where you think the spirit is most likely to be. Drums are beaten and sacrifices performed at this spot. Spirits enjoy a sacrifice of sheep or pigs.

As a sorceress, you spend most of your time conducting ceremonies and purifying the things around you. You may pray or dance during sacrifices or work to wipe out evil spirits. You're very useful in times of drought since you know how to lead dances that ask the gods for rain. Sometimes the emperor employs you to worship various gods on his behalf.

You can conjure spirits by invocation (calling on them to appear) or incantation (repeating specific words or sounds). You might even surrender your body as a medium to the spirits. (Just make sure they're renting the space, not moving in.) Some people will request your services in addition to those of doctors to cure a disease. Some unethical sorceresses (not you, surely) also perform "black magic" by cursing others or making an image of someone and burying it to cause that person harm. Don't be tempted—those accused of practicing black magic have been put to death.

Hear me, great spirit of the rains.

Buddhist Monk or Nun

You lead a life of meditation and mindfulness, having pledged not to kill living things. Ideally, you can't work the fields because digging, irrigating, and harvesting crops could mean accidentally killing something living, like the beetle in the soil just beside your pitchfork. So how does your monastery survive? Everyone, from the emperor right down to the peasants, donates to monasteries. A gift is thought to redeem sins they've committed in this lifetime. A sizable donation can even help out dead relatives, causing them to be reborn to a higher station.

Because of all of these donations, monasteries own a lot of land and hire tenant farmers to work it. The monks themselves handle money lending and pawnbroking. Monks don't charge interest to poor farmers who need seed, though they will claim a valuable object (like an iron cauldron) as security. People of higher status who need a loan, however, *are* charged interest—often as high as 120 percent. (That's worse than credit cards.) You and your fellow monks or nuns make good money off the rich. But most of the monastery's income goes back into the community as charity.

Shaolin Warrior Monk

As a devout Buddhist, you know that you should not engage in violence or warfare. That's also why you are a vegetarian. And yet, you are a highly skilled warrior. Shaolin kung fu may have developed as a way to keep your temple safe from bandits—the temple's coffers are filled with donations from the richest nobles around. Though it might seem like a contradiction, you and many other monks feel that martial arts, like meditation, is a tool to bring about spiritual awareness. After all, kung fu requires dedication and complete focus.

You have practiced kung fu since you came to the Shaolin temple at the age of four. Your training covers the 72 arts of kung fu. You've learned how to use anything as a weapon, including chopsticks, needles, coins, and small fans. You strike 1,000 layers of thick paper over and over again for years, until your hits are as swift as rain drops in a storm.

Your training takes almost every moment of your time for decades. By the time you are done, you might be as good as a famous monk like Jue Yuan, who could break stone slabs with his fists, crush pebbles into powder in his palms, and knock a hollow in the wall with his finger. Or perhaps, like Shu Ran, you will master the art of the "light body" and be able to leap out of one pit into another or jump over high walls. Other monks have managed to defeat enemies in complete darkness or beat off arrows that were shot at them. Shaolin monks seem to have almost supernatural abilities—no wonder the training is so hard and long. You are a lethal pacifist, and your temple will go down in legends and lore for thousands of years to come.

Chapter 6

Life, Death, and Well-being Jobs

If you fell sick in imperial China, you had a good chance of getting the treatment you needed, especially if you lived in a large city. The medical system was based on empirical observation and rigorous training, so treatment was quite effective and safe. After thousands of years of ministering to people with herbs, acupuncture, massage, diet, and exercise, doctors had learned quite a bit. In 600 BCE, the state had even set aside 17 hectares (42 acres) of the best land in the capital for medical gardens. There were 656 officially recognized medicinal substances, which included animal and mineral products. Treatments were available for just about everything, although surgery was relatively rare. It did happen on occasion, though. In some cases, doctors even managed to reattach body parts successfully.

From birth to death, there were professionals to ease people's transitions through major life events. On the health front, there were practitioners like doctors, acupuncturists, wet nurses, and midwives. Physiognomists and matchmakers guided people when they needed to make big decisions affecting their lives. Are you the kind of person who will dedicate your life to helping other people get on with theirs? If so, you'll find the perfect job here.

Doctor

Unlike the Europeans, you follow methods that have a long history of success. No bloodletting or leeches for you! This profession, open to men and women, is one of the few jobs that can make women wealthy, especially if they treat noblewomen or the ladies of the imperial court. Some female doctors own their own clinics or drugstores.

As a doctor, you strive to keep the two natural forces of yin and yang balanced in your patients. You take the patient's pulse in six different places. Some people call going to the doctor "going to have my pulse felt." You smell patients' breath, observe how they look, and ask about their medical history. Some very dedicated doctors have even been known to smell (or taste!) their patient's poop. You pay attention to how your patients are sitting and walking, to their voice, to their hair. You ask about their daily life: family, living conditions, food, sleep, emotions, and physical activity. If a patient is a wealthy merchant or noble, you also check his or her medical records (only the rich can afford to keep records). Then you write out a prescription. Your prescriptions aren't just for medicine—you may also prescribe a special diet or certain exercises.

EXORCISM
For as long as there has been ancestor worship in China, there's also been exorcism. Colorful scary masks are worn by dancers as they shoo away the evil spirits that can cause death and disease. Dancers often wear red and black robes, and they engage in fierce and intense dancing, trying to mimic the movements of tigers or other ferocious animals.

Medical Professor

You work for the Office of Supreme Medicine, which is both the public institution for doctors and their college. The office keeps track of the healing records of medics, doctors, acupuncturists, master masseurs, and practitioners of massage, offering them merits for everyone they've cured.

You are a professor at this distinguished institution. You teach in one of four departments, along with an assistant professor: the department of general medicine, the department of acupuncture, the department of massage/exercises, or the department of exorcism (incantations, visualizations, and hand gestures).

There's much to teach aspiring young doctors, and you'll be testing them with eight-part examinations. You also want to instill in your students the ethical precepts of your professions. Like you, they must pledge to be compassionate and willing to treat anyone, must stay on call at all times, must give up striving for material gain, must be well learned, and must be precise and accurate in their judgments. It's a tall order, but your students are eager to try.

Acupuncturist

You work with needles, but you're not giving out vaccines. If someone's yin and yang are out of whack, you'll try to restore the balance. You treat people for all sorts of problems, everything from chronic pain to constipation. You insert needles or place heat or pressure in specific places on the patient's body to help restore the proper flow of *qi*, or life energy. The needles don't hurt, since they're made from very thin pieces of metal. Before metal, they were made from bone and stone.

Acupuncture is an ancient tradition. The Yellow Emperor (a half-historical, half-legendary figure who was supposed to have reigned from 2696 to 2598 BCE) is credited with writing a book about it, *The Yellow Emperor's Classic of Internal Medicine*. Though we may never know who actually wrote the book, it's one of the earliest recorded documents on medicine. Far in the future, doctors and scientists will have a hard time figuring out exactly how acupuncture works. You and your patients just know that it does.

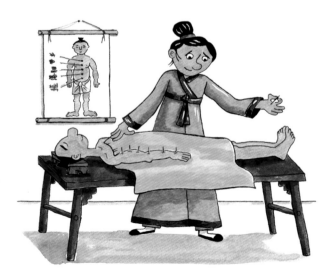

Midwife

You're probably a mother yourself, and your clients call you "great aunt" or "granny" to show their respect. People in your community know and trust you. You've learned your skills through your own experience with pregnancy and birth, as well as through an apprenticeship. Birthing is a woman's domain. Sometimes male doctors are called in, but they are not allowed in the birthing room. You are the one who helps a mother bring her child into the world.

Midwives don't need to get a license or pass a test to practice their trade. If you're a village midwife, you likely can't read or write, though you're very skilled. As a midwife or female doctor of the imperial court, you would receive more formal training. You might be an official palace slave, probably between the ages of 15 and 25, who was sent to medical school at the imperial court. There, you would learn about calming the fetus, helping a woman in childbirth, nursing wounds, and using acupuncture. Your schooling can take between two and seven years, depending on the subject you study. If you pass your exams at the end, you'll treat royalty in a respected profession.

Calm down, wee one. You'll be with us soon.

Wet Nurse

Physiognomist

Go ahead and judge a book by its cover. It's your job to evaluate people based on their appearance. You might be called in to foretell a baby's future or to see if a concubine is worthy of the emperor. You look very carefully at your subject's face. Does a woman have a big chin? If so, she's going to have many children and grandchildren. You'll also look at the face as a whole. What animal does your subject look like? Do her facial features remind you of a tiger? Uh-oh—that's a sign she'll be ruthless and cruel. If someone has a phoenix's neck or dragon eyes, then you're staring into the face of nobility. You pay attention to the subject's aura and *qi*. You judge your subjects by their body size, too. A thin person is probably nasty, treacherous, and mean to his or her parents.

Your work can help people to live in harmony with their inner natures. But your judgments and predictions have serious consequences.

They can affect people's marriages, their jobs, and the direction of their lives. Officials and nobles could be elevated, dismissed, or even killed based on what you think of their looks.

Many rich women don't have the time or the inclination to breastfeed their children. That's where you come in. You need to be healthy—parents are warned against hiring wet nurses with maladies like goiters, swellings, eczema, scabies, baldness, stuffy noses, deafness, and body odor. Deodorant on this job interview is a must! Often, a wet nurse will nurse a child for years. You may be responsible for raising the kid as well. Not surprisingly, children often feel closer to their wet nurses than they do to their own mothers. This can be a good thing for you. Two emperors ennobled their wet nurses, and the most renowned master of prose in the Tang Dynasty, Han Yu, kept his wet nurse as part of his household for her entire life. During festivals, he and his wife and children would all pay their respects to her on bended knee. Who says kids aren't grateful?

Veterinarian

Professional Wailer

The first people to ply the veterinary trade were priests. They were believed to possess healing powers that could vanquish the evil spirits plaguing both people and animals. All medical treatment initially was offered by "priest doctors." Priests who specialized in healing animals were known as "horse priests," "cow priests," and so on. As medical treatments advanced, veterinarians began to treat animals based on the principles of yin and yang. Veterinarians prescribe herbs and perform acupuncture on animals in order to heal them. There are books on the treatment of camels, cattle, and donkeys, but the majority of books written focus exclusively on horses. By the time of the Tang Dynasty, the government realized that it needed good vets for all the army horses, so it created a department of veterinary medicine and established a school of veterinary medicine. As a veterinarian, you are considered a little less important than a doctor, but you hold down a good job and are respected within your community.

This is an equal opportunity profession: both men and women work as wailers, but you have to be good at lamenting. You work on call for a funeral parlor, along with the masked, square-faced exorcists who expel demons at graves for a fee. Your employer also rents out hearses and other equipment. Your job is to keen loudly during the funeral procession, so crocodile tears are a real asset in your line of work. You might even sing a dirge. If you're good, you'll have people weeping with grief at your song. You're there to maintain a mood of sorrow. No one would accuse you of putting the "fun" in "funeral."

My treatment will put you back in the saddle again.

Matchmaker

> Don't be scared! Get married for your families.

Everyone who gets married needs a matchmaker, and this is one profession not open to men. As a matchmaker, you need to get close to the prospective bride so that you can report on her looks and her health to the family of the prospective groom. She must be old enough to get married. (Girls can be married at 12, boys at 14.) She can't be half the age of the groom or younger. Nor can she be related to him in any way. The definition of incest extends as far as marrying a fourth cousin on the father's side, and it's also forbidden to marry anyone who shares the same surname. The punishment for an infraction could be 100 blows with a thick rod, penal servitude for a year, or exile to a district 1,340 kilometers (833 miles) away.

As a matchmaker, you're not really worried about matching up two people; rather, you're matching up two families. The bride and groom have little say about whom they want to marry, or even what they're looking for in a spouse. Sometimes families will also marry off one of their kids to a ghost—the soul of someone who has died. That way, the two families are still linked through marriage, and the soul of their loved one will not be alone. It might seem spooky, but if you're married to a ghost, the two of you will probably argue less than most married couples do.

Chapter 7

Law & Order and Military Jobs

At first, the law in ancient China was all about set punishments for set actions. It didn't matter who broke the law or why they did it—the punishment was the same. Let's say your parents followed this system now: you'd always get a time out for hitting your sister, whether you smacked her because she was annoying or because there was a huge blackfly on her back. Later on, Confucianism started to influence theories of the law. They began to extend leniency based on things like virtue, ability, and status. Not everyone was equal before the law. If you were related to the emperor or were a high-ranking civil servant, you might be asked to give up your position instead of being punished. The law was strictly preserved in legal code.

Laws were set by the emperor and administered by civil servants. In cases that involved the death penalty, the emperor had to give his permission for the penalty to be carried out. Nobody could be convicted of a crime without confessing. Unfortunately for suspects, the use of torture to obtain a confession was allowed.

Magistrate

You uphold the law and make sure people don't go unpunished for their crimes. Royal decree has it that the walls of your office be inscribed with all the laws of land. That way, even when you're taking a tea break you have nothing else to look at. When you sentence someone, there are five major punishments to choose from: thrashing with a thin rod, thrashing with a thick rod, penal servitude, exile, and execution.

You'll assign thrashing with a thin rod for acts like failing to report a fire or making an illegal entry into someone's home. Thrashing with a thick rod is for more serious offenses, like pulling out a square inch or more of an adversary's hair during a fight.

Penal servitude is for crimes such as peeking into the imperial palace or, as an artisan, refusing orders to paint the imperial boat. This will mean digging imperial graves (men) or sewing for the court (women) for one to three years.

The fourth level of punishment, exile, can mean being sent 1,071, 1,340, or 1,609 kilometers (666, 833, or 1,000 miles) away from home. A person can be exiled for making false accusations or for stealing armor or a crossbow. One man was exiled for putting together a joke book. (Or maybe it was a book of criminally bad puns?)

Execution is saved for 233 of the most heinous crimes, including falsely accusing your grandparents, kidnapping and then selling someone into slavery, and opening and desecrating a tomb.

As a magistrate, you don't only sentence people; you're also a bit of an interrogator. You conduct each hearing over three days. On the first day, you take the suspect's statement. On the second and third days, you question the suspect based on those statements using five ancient principles for interrogation.

Minister of Justice

Prefect

Your influence over legal matters is second only to that of the emperor. Among your other powers, you dispense general amnesties. That means, if you like, you can let people off the hook for their crimes. You're in charge of upholding, administering, and interpreting the law. If the provincial judges can't agree on a difficult case, it comes to you for final judgment. You recommend changes to the laws as well. Your ministry also maintains the imperial prison. Trials are conducted at this prison, and executions, too. No wonder everyone defers to you.

Your title is "prefect," and you report to the magistrate. You're really the chief of police, since you're in charge of all the subprefects in your district. You and your team work together to fight crime and to gather evidence against murderers, robbers, and other criminals.

There's been some pretty impressive detective work to date in China. And later, Chinese law enforcers will be the first to practice forensic entomology. In 1235, when a villager was stabbed to death, the authorities ordered everyone to gather in the town square and surrender their sickles. All of the sickles looked the same to the naked eye, but only one attracted a swarm of blow flies, which could detect traces of blood. The guilty sickle owner confessed. Great police work!

Gold Bird Guard

You patrol the cities, making sure everyone is conducting their business in an orderly fashion. This isn't a one-sheriff situation, though—far from it. Every intersection has a police post, with 30 guards stationed at major crossroads and 5 at minor ones. Between 20 and 100 guards are also posted at the city gates to control who leaves and who enters. Even though the roads are wide and well maintained, accidents can still happen when people race their horses through the crowd. You're ready to take out either your thin or your thick rod to punish the speeder on the spot. Only doctors on emergency calls or imperial messengers will avoid the wrath of the Gold Bird Guards, and your peck is definitely worse than your chirp.

Market Commandant

You're a government official who puts in long days making sure that everything is fair and square in the crowded, noisy market, where everyone is trying to get the best price for their crops and wares. At least the market is well organized. Every lane is devoted to a single good: meat, medicine, axes, steamed buns, fish, or ready-made clothes. At your office in the middle of the market, you stay busy inspecting weights and measures, looking for counterfeit coins, and weeding out goods that don't meet the imperial standard for size, weight, and quality of materials or workmanship. No one is going to sell a shoddy plow on your watch.

To prevent price fixing and other unfair practices by merchants, you set the prevailing prices for all commodities every 10 days. Beware of trying to cut yourself a deal, though. If the government finds out that you dropped the price of axes just before picking up a nice new axe for yourself, you'll be out of a job and have to repay the merchant twice the original price.

Military Service— Conscripted

Are you a man between the ages of 23 and 56? Congratulations—you've just been conscripted for two years of working for the army. If you have enough cash on hand, you can buy your way out of military service. If you're a peasant, you'll likely serve your time in the infantry.

As a soldier, you get food (not very good food, though), clothing (just enough), and equipment, but no pay. Out of the rations you're allowed, you can draw some portions of grain for your family. The amount of grain you receive depends on your status and on the age and sex of your family members.

Some generals work their infantrymen all day and night with sentry duty. Others take a more laissez-faire attitude, favoring time to relax and little formal organization. You can probably guess which kind of general is more popular.

As a soldier you could be doing anything from running messages or cooking to building bricks. Some conscripted farmers are forced to march miles to a watchtower, only to end up farming for the army. Once you're done your two years, you're free again—until you get drafted for your two years in the government's labor force, that is.

Female Warrior

Even though there is no room for you in the army, you won't let that stop you. War is traditionally a man's game, but you are strong, smart, and capable. You might have been brought up as a lowly singing girl, or maybe you're a princess. Either way, when no one else could do the job, women stepped in. Princess Pingyang led the "Army of the Lady" into a rebellion during the Tang Dynasty, capturing cities and inciting 70,000 men to join her cause. Lady Fu Hao started out as a slave, one of several wives to a king. She was skilled in martial and military arts and quickly rose to power, leading top generals and thousands of troops. Her husband had nothing but the greatest respect for her. When she died, she was buried with battle axes and other weapons so that when she got to the afterworld, everyone would recognize her status as a top general and warrior. Her husband honored her spirit by offering sacrifices and asking for her spiritual assistance in battles. Like her, you may be recognized for bravery and military skill long after you're gone.

Watchtower Guard, Great Wall

You're moving up in the world. Literally. Now that you've labored for years building the Great Wall, you get to climb up top and guard it. From high up, you can see if any of those pesky barbarians are planning a raid. You might think guarding a wall would be a pretty easy job, but your company commander is always on your back. You're living in cramped quarters, and army food deserves its terrible reputation. You freeze in the winter, and you bake in the summer. Keep your eyes peeled, though, even in the stinging sand storms that create a "dry fog." You have to sweep the sand every day to make sure that if anyone tries to sneak up you'll see their footprints. You also need to stock up on stuff to

burn. If there's danger, you need to light a beacon fire. If you spot a group of fewer than 500 raiders, you light one column of smoke. If you see what looks like 500 to 3,000 raiders, get two columns on the go. For more than that (uh-oh) light up three columns fast.

Your signal is noticed immediately, since the guard towers are within view of each other all along the Great Wall. It's like a giant game of "telephone." What should you burn? If you find wood around that's great, but the best fuel is dried wolf dung. It burns black, so its smoke is seen most clearly. It's also handy for stuffing inside a paper bag, which you can light and leave on a Mongol's doorstep. (Just kidding.)

 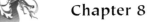

Chapter 8

Peasant Jobs

If you lived in ancient China, you were probably a peasant. Almost everyone was. It wasn't a job many of us would choose. People valued what you did, but you worked long, long days, you felt like your back was breaking, and you only ever had just enough money to keep from starving. You made sure you worshipped your ancestors. You wanted them to put in a good word for you with the gods to prevent terrible disasters like droughts or floods. If something destroyed your crops, you were really in for it.

If your family was lucky enough to own a small piece of land, it was probably only the top bit. This was called having "topsoil" rights. Your landlord had the "subsoil" rights. As long as he paid taxes, he had a permanent claim to the land. He wasn't allowed to work it himself, though, so you paid him a fixed rent or gave him part of what you grew. In return, you got to live on the land, farm it, and even sell or lease the topsoil rights to someone else. You probably didn't do that, though, because your land provided the food you ate. You were just thankful you could afford that top inch of dirt.

Female Peasant

Is there anything you *can't* do? You make the clothes, cook the meals, care for the spiritual health of your family, keep your in-laws happy, and help in the fields. You are the backbone of your family, and if it weren't for you, your kids, husband, and in-laws wouldn't have a stitch to wear. You weave tunics, trousers, hats, rain capes, and even sandals from whatever material you have, usually hemp and rice straw. You must never waste fuel. Chop up everything into small pieces so that it cooks quickly, and stack steamers on top of each other—you can't afford to waste steam, either. You probably don't cook much meat, if any. When your family gets sick, you gather herbs and nurse them back to health. You live in a small hut with three generations: your in-laws, your husband, and your kids. It's crowded, but you always pay proper respect to your parents-in-law. If you don't, they can order your husband to divorce you.

CHORES FOR CHILDREN

Peasant children start work early. If their family is fortunate enough to own a few animals (maybe some chickens, ducks, pigs, sheep, or an oxen to pull the plow), then it's up to the children to help feed them and to keep everything clean. Boys and girls are also expected to be in the fields pulling weeds and assisting where they can. Boys would love the chance to go to school and maybe one day become a civil servant, creating a better life for themselves and their families. But only a very, very few peasant boys will ever get the opportunity to study classics and math all day. They're kept busy cleaning the pig pen and doing other chores.

Male Peasant

Your livelihood depends on the weather. If you live in the north of China, your crops are mainly wheat and millet. If you live in the south, you grow fields of rice. You own topsoil rights to your small farm, but you worry. A flood or a drought can destroy an entire year of work. Even if your crop is ruined, you'll still need to pay taxes. When the weather isn't great, you face some tough choices. You can sell what you own, but you don't own much, mainly tools to help you farm. If you borrow money and then have another bad year, you'll lose what little land you have. You'll have to become a tenant farmer, one of the few jobs worse than peasant farmer. You love your kids, but they're hard to feed, and you might be forced to sell them into slavery. You carry a heavy load. It's a hard life, and there's always the chance it could get harder.

Break for tea, Dad.

Endless Chain Worker

Another dry summer.

Not much rain falls on your crops. When you're growing rice, though, you need plenty of water so you can flood your fields. Since you depend on your family farm, you had better hop on the "dragon's backbones," also known as the endless chain. And wow, is this work ever endless. The chain pump is operated by the foot power of two people, like a giant treadmill, and it scoops up water from the rivers or streams. Find a partner you like because the two of you will often spend all day on the machine, redirecting enough water from the river to irrigate your farm and maybe even your whole village. Well, at least you won't need a gym membership to stay fit. You'll have plenty of time to chat about the weather, too, as in *Do you think it'll rain soon?*

Night Soil Spreader

Cormorant Fisher

You don't need a fishing pole or a net. You have fishing birds! Cormorants—large, black water birds—are expert divers and fish catchers. You attach a snare around the neck of your bird, a tight necklace that means it won't be able to swallow large fish. You and your bird work together. You paddle your boat to a good fishing spot and, on your hand signal, the bird dives into the water. Almost every time, your cormorant will come up with a lovely silver fish in its beak. The bird returns to the boat, where you make it spit out its catch and then put the fish in a floating net by your boat to keep it fresh. You'll keep most of the fish, but you'll also slice off some manageable bites to reward your fishing fowl.

You have the stinkiest job in all of China. At least you're not alone; someone has to do this dirty job for every farming family. You gather up the smelly pots and use a ladle to scoop out the poop and spread it over the fields. You may not find it appetizing right now, but your poop will feed the soil and help produce tastier crops. If your family owns animals, you'll use their poop as well. Waste not, want not!

Silk Maker

You are a woman who works all day, cooking, cleaning, looking after the children, and taking directions from your husband and your husband's parents. But you're also in charge of a very important secret: how to make silk. This secret has been kept from countries outside China for hundreds of years.

To make a little extra money, you raise caterpillars. You feed them fresh mulberry leaves every day. You know everything about their life cycle—these little silk worms are worth a lot to you. You watch the caterpillar spin a thick cocoon out of a single thread. When your caterpillar is done spinning, you drop the cocoon into boiling water. Too bad for the insect inside! The boiling water loosens the cocoon, and then you unravel it in one long filament. You clean that and spin it into a very strong thread.

The silk you make is so valuable that people often use it in place of money. Rich people wear silk all the time. Romans adore it, too. When their whole empire eventually goes broke, it's partly because they've exchanged so much gold for your fine, soft material. Talk about slaves to fashion! But be careful whom you talk to—if you tell any foreign visitors the secret of making silk, you'll be put to death!

Chapter 9

Corvée Labor, Convict Labor, and Slavery Jobs

If you were in the corvée labor corps, you were a peasant whose time had come up. Every able-bodied man had to put in time doing hard labor for the government, unless he was rich enough to pay a fee to get out of it. Otherwise it was a long two years.

Criminals who did hard labor expected to eventually return to their families, if they didn't die first. Some criminals even signed up for hard labor, after conviction, since it provided partial freedom and could advance their status. That was the good part. Other than that, hard labor was *all* bad. You could have been sent to the mines (iron, copper, or salt), or to dig a massive grave, or maybe to work on the Great Wall. You might have been forced to build roads in the mountains, where one misstep could have meant a very long fall. Some convicts were kept bound in iron chains. Hopefully the emperor was in a generous mood, as only he could offer general amnesty to criminals. That usually happened at least once a year.

If you were a slave, you remained captive for life, unless the emperor offered a full-scale manumission (which he did sometimes, freeing everyone from slavery).

THE GREAT WALL OF CHINA

The Great Wall of China deserves its name: it stretches 8,851.8 kilometers (5,500 miles) long. (For a shorter stroll, you could try walking across Canada—that's only about 5,000 kilometers [3,100 miles] from the Atlantic to the Pacific.) It look a long time to build the wall: workers started in the 5th century BCE and continued maintaining and expanding it right through to the 16th century. It's estimated that over a million people died while constructing the wall.

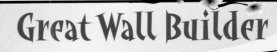

Great Wall Builder

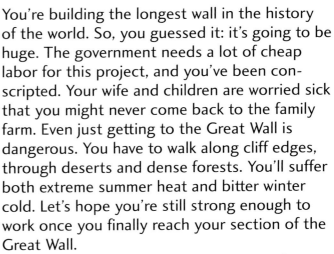

You're building the longest wall in the history of the world. So, you guessed it: it's going to be huge. The government needs a lot of cheap labor for this project, and you've been conscripted. Your wife and children are worried sick that you might never come back to the family farm. Even just getting to the Great Wall is dangerous. You have to walk along cliff edges, through deserts and dense forests. You'll suffer both extreme summer heat and bitter winter cold. Let's hope you're still strong enough to work once you finally reach your section of the Great Wall.

The Great Wall is constructed mainly from what's around: earth, gravel, and stones. It needs to be even along the top and has to be built to a certain height, about 5 meters (5.5 yards). You and your fellow workers, poor farmers and criminals, erect a frame made of wood and then fill it. You shovel in huge amounts of sand, earth, and clay, tamping the pile down as you go. Your section of the wall is made from rammed earth. On other sections of the wall, workers use large stones instead, which means a massive amount of heavy lifting.

Fresh workers are continually needed because so many people die on the job. If you drop dead while piling on the sand and dirt, your coworkers won't bother lifting you out. They'll just heap more dirt on top of you and make you a part of the wall.

Grave Digger

Salt Mine Worker

This is such a grueling job, there's a good chance it'll be your last. The grave you're digging isn't the 1.8-meters (6-feet)-deep, just-enough-room-for-one-person type. You're digging a grave in advance for the emperor and he's planning to go out in style. He lives in a palace surrounded by the finest of the fine, and that's how he wants to spend the rest of eternity, too. So not only do you have to dig enough room for an entire palace, you might also have to dig underground rivers filled with quicksilver (mercury).

If the emperor dies during your hard-labor stint, he'll be laid to rest among countless treasures in a beautiful palace, and then you and your coworkers will have to bury the whole thing. Many of the crew will die from exhaustion and overwork. But hey, since they're creating a hole anyway, anyone who falls over dead will just be pushed into the pit. Talk about digging your own grave.

Almost everyone in China has the same diet, filling up on cereals like millet, rice, or wheat (not Froot Loops) and vegetables. You can't stay healthy without at least some salt, however, and salt can be hard to get. If you live by the ocean, salt is there for the taking, but otherwise it has to be mined out of the earth. Since salt is so precious and in such high demand—millions of people need it to survive—it's very, very valuable.

Salt mining requires serious engineering skill. First, somebody has to drill over 600 meters (650 yards) into the earth. Mineral deposits are brought to the surface in long, tubular buckets. (Bamboo is perfect for this.) The buckets are raised and lowered using a winding gear and a pulley. Hauling up bucket after bucket of heavy salt sludge is probably not your idea of a good time. The sludge goes through a bamboo pipeline into sheltered pans, where it is dried out until only the salt remains. Sometimes, to hurry up the process, fires are lit under the pans. Since the mines are in the desert, there's not much wood around. Bamboo tubes full of natural gas feed the fires.

Litter Attendant

How's your upper-body strength? This is an equal opportunity job, since litters are sometimes carried by palace ladies, sometimes by slaves or servants. A litter is a chair or a bed that is hoisted up on horizontal poles. It takes two or more people to lift and carry one—this is a job where you definitely want coworkers. Litters are used to transport the rich or injured people. The emperor alone has 57 bearers.

Sometimes he will use his litter just to get around the palace. ("Litter! I want to be carried to my bath!") Deluxe models are nice for the person being carried, since they have canopies, curtained cabs, and sometimes large chairs. These heavy, fancy litters aren't so great for your back, though. Let's hope most of your work will involve trips around the palace instead of a trek over the mountains.

Dark Green Head

Government Slave

You're a cut above when it comes to slaves. Your name doesn't come from the actual color of your head, but rather from the color of the head scarf you wear: blue-green. As a dark green head, you fall into the "lucky slave" category. You are skilled and won't have to dirty your hands with manual labor. You may be trusted enough to visit the court on your master's behalf. You're smooth in your manner and eloquent, and you understand the ways of the palace. There might even be a time when someone high up likes your work so much he or she gives you a cash reward. Some dark green heads become rich, and they're allowed to keep their money and spend it however they wish.

As far as slavery goes, you're not in the worst position. Most government slaves work in the palace, tend animals, do office work, or ply a skilled trade like making farm tools. Female slaves could be entertainers, wet nurses, or domestic servants for the women of the imperial family. As a government slave, you're in a better position than most peasants.

If you're a child slave it's for one of three reasons. Maybe your parents were too poor to feed you. Or your dad or mom (most likely your dad) committed a serious crime, like treason, and now your whole family has been "confiscated" by the government, along with all your worldly goods. Or you could have been born to a slave, which means you're a slave from the minute you take your first breath.

You have to obey your master, and you're considered his property, but your master doesn't have total power over you. He can't kill you, and there are government laws about providing slaves with enough to eat, as well as with decent shelter. Unless the emperor issues one of his periodic orders to free all slaves, however, you'll never have a say in where you live or what you do.

 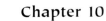 

Chapter 10

Artisans and Performers

As an artisan or a performer, your rank in society was just below that of a peasant. Financially, you were probably better off than a farmer, but not necessarily by much. Your income and how people saw you depended on your level of skill and what you did. You might have made crude pots for peasants, or you could have been a master artisan who worked for the government sculpting life-like statues of a huge army. If you were a performer, you put in long hours practicing. Even if you performed in the opera, there was no exclusive dressing room or star treatment for you. Artisans weren't banned from becoming officials, but they were often lumped together with merchants, so there was not a lot of respect headed your way. The government wasn't too keen on traveling performers because it felt they distracted farmers from their important work and tapped into their almost bare wallets. You had to make a living, though, so you got out to the market and started promoting your talents.

Opera Actor

You were picked to be an opera actor when you were just a little kid. Ever since your parents signed a seven-year contract for you, you've been in training. Your teacher is the one paying for all your food and rent, so you're picking up a pretty hefty debt along the way. You'll pay him back when you start earning money through your performances. In the meantime, you get up at five a.m. for exercises, and then spend the rest of the day learning acting, combat skills, and acrobatics. There's as much martial arts in your training as there is opera singing, so you're exhausted by the end of the day. And of course, the end of the day is just when you have to perform for the public! If anyone in your troupe makes a mistake, you'll all be beaten with bamboo canes.

Your sets are simple, but that's okay because the audience can use their imaginations. They know that when you flick a whip on stage you're pretending to be riding a horse. A table can represent a city wall, a mountain, or a bed. Your makeup, on the other hand, is hugely elaborate. Be prepared to spend a lot of time applying it, because your colorful face paint shows your audience what kind of character you are playing.

Once you're trained for the opera, you're not qualified for much else. You didn't get any academic schooling, and you've got to pay back your debt. Like this job or not, thanks to your parents, you're stuck in it now.

Acrobat

Musician

You perform at markets and on special occasions at the imperial court. You might be a slave who has shown promise or a poor peasant with ability. You started your training when you were five. You and your fellow performers juggle, eat fire, swallow knives, and perform amazing feats of balance and strength. Some of what you do is death-defying. Tightrope walkers, almost always women, wear wooden platform shoes or tie long stilts to their shins. (As if your job really needs to be any harder.) There are also daring pole acts, in which an anchorwoman balances a painted pole 20 to 30 meters (70 to 100 feet) in height on her head. The pole has a crossbar on top, and young girls do acrobatics there, hanging by their chins or doing handstands and somersaults. The emperor may summon your troupe to the palace to dazzle visiting foreigners. Mostly, though, you and your fellow acrobats entertain at the busy market, carving out a little elbow room to swallow your sword between the fish sellers and the squawking poultry.

You are a woman who comes from a modest background. Your family are farmers or maybe merchants, but your great talent has you performing for rich nobles and maybe even the emperor. Musicians tend to be women, and you sing or play a variety of instruments: flute, panpipes, mouth organ, zither, or drums. Yours is a job with potential. Quite a few empresses were musicians when they first caught the emperor's eye and ear. On the downside, sometimes musicians are buried with nobles to entertain them in the afterworld. That's the kind of job security you don't want.

Printer

Printing takes a long time. You used to carve out every single page on a piece of wood. You would trace the original text, then carve around the words so that the characters stood out. This was extra tricky, since you were creating a mirror image of the text. Once a page was carved, you would wet it with ink and then press a sheet of paper over top, turning out as many copies of each page as you needed. When you were finished printing that particular book, though, the woodblocks you'd created were essentially useless. Your job got a lot easier when Bi Sheng invented movable type. Now you can place the characters where you need them to be inked and copied. Of course, it's still a heck of a lot of work to do the initial carving. For one book, *Records of Jingde County*, the printer needed to carve 30,000 individual characters.

You're tired of seeing your carved wood blocks wear down from repeated use, so you're glad when people start to cast more durable type from bronze, copper, iron, and tin. It's still a ton of work, but it's faster than carving everything by hand.

Paper Maker

You might make high-quality material for calligraphers or rough rice-straw paper—the world's first toilet paper. Of course, the royal family would never use the rough toilet paper. Theirs is custom-made, tinted yellow, and perfumed. The process of making paper is a secret kept from foreigners. Don't let your recipe for toilet paper slip out, or you could be beheaded.

Making paper takes a lot of heat and muscle. You also need to keep up with the times—methods and materials keep changing and improving. The first paper was made from a combination of plants, rags, and even fishing nets. But now, by gradual trial and error, you've learned you can make a reliable paper from materials like rice straw, bamboo, hemp, or birch leaves. You soak and boil your materials, then pound them into a pulp in water. (This takes a lot of strength—bamboo and hemp are tough to break down with a mortar and pestle.) Next, you spread the pulp onto a bamboo screen and let it dry into a stiff sheet. The first papers were thick and strong enough (thank you, fish nets) to be used for clothes, curtains, and sometimes even light armor!

Poet

You know your profession is well respected when it's one of the "three perfections," along with calligraphy and painting. Poetry has been popular for a very long time, and it's evolved in different ways. It used to be sung or chanted to musical accompaniment, but now people also enjoy simply reading your verses. Your words are so beautiful they'll be recreated on silk by the most skilled calligraphers. Painters will try to evoke what you've written, and you may be inspired by a painting yourself. Before the Tang Dynasty it was mostly men and princesses who wrote poetry, but if you're living in the Tang Dynasty, the golden age of poetry, you're one of many women writing. Shangguan Wan'er was a slave during the Tang Dynasty who was smart, studied hard, and also wrote poems. The empress came across one of her poems when Shangguan was only 13 years old. The empress was so impressed that, even though she had ordered the killing of Shangguan's father and grandfather, she elevated Shangguan to the position of imperial secretary. Poetry—what a practical skill for getting ahead.

Calligrapher

You're more of an artist than a writer. In fact, it's natural for calligraphers to write out someone else's poem. You don't write with a pen or pencil, but with a brush made from soft animal hairs. Everything you do has to be perfect.

It's important that your ink be just the right consistency and color. One master says you can get five colors from black ink alone. When you're ready to work, there will be no elbows on the table. You hold your brush straight up (watching to see that your long sleeves don't drag in the ink).

Chinese writing uses a logographic system. That means it's composed of symbols, each of which represents an entire spoken word. The symbols don't give you any hints about how to pronounce the word, so everything has to be memorized. Rather than the 26 letters of the alphabet, you have to learn thousands of characters, and each one must be shaped using specific brush strokes executed in a strict order. Some characters take up to 26 brushstrokes to create. It takes years of practice to infuse your calligraphy with the right life force, or *qi*, and with the qualities of energy, strength, and movement.

Ink Stick Maker

Painter

You can't create five different shades of black using barbarian liquid ink. Serious artists insist on ink sticks. Your sticks allow the user to control both color and consistency by adding just the right amount of water to the ink stone before grinding.

To make your ink sticks, you combine pine soot and glue. (Your glue could be made of egg whites, fish skin, or animal hide.) To make an ink stick extra special, you might add medicines or herbs, like sandalwood, or even pearl dust. All the ingredients are mixed together in precise portions and then kneaded like dough. The dough is cut, pressed into a mold, and then allowed to dry slowly. The molds are often very elaborate, making the ink stick a beautiful work of art in itself. It takes at least three months to produce one small ink stick, but it's worth it. Your skill deepens with time, and it's no wonder that what you craft is considered one of the four treasures of study: ink stick, ink stone, writing brush, and paper.

You're a rich aristocrat or an accomplished scholar/official who has the time and the leisure to paint. You use the same tools as a calligrapher: brush, ink stick, ink stone, and either silk or paper. You paint on scrolls, which can be rolled up for easy transport and hung to display. Depending on the dynasty during which you live, you might concentrate on painting either people or landscapes. The people you depict might be graceful aristocrats involved in court life or figures illustrating a Confucian moral, like a good wife's behavior toward her in-laws. Either way, you're trying to convey the vitality of your subjects, and your paintings must have an energy of their own. Oddly, many of them will likely end up underground. Art is so highly valued that the rich often order it placed in their graves. That way, they can continue to appreciate it in the afterlife.

Bronze Worker

You know how to combine copper and tin into bronze. While many of the items you make are plain (not that the farmer minds—he just appreciates that his tools work), the dishes and goblets you design for religious rituals and for rich buyers are amazing. You often inlay the bronze with beautiful designs or inscriptions in gold or silver so that your bowls and cups look more like sculptures. Animals (real and imagined) are a popular theme, so you decorate vessels with intertwining images of elephants, birds, tigers, and dragons. Mirrors made of highly polished bronze are also in demand: one side is for gazing at yourself, and the other side is ornamented. These ornaments can be decorative, but sometimes they are considered magical. There's also a great need for bronze coins and weapons, so you might have secured a government job in one of the factories that makes these for the state.

Illusionist

You have a lot of tricks up your sleeves. There are different types of illusionists. Some want to convert people to their religion, and others just want to make a bit of money in markets and villages. One magician was said to cut off his tongue, put the bloody stump in a bowl to be passed around the audience, and then reattach the tongue in front of everyone. Another, a Taoist priest named Ye, would call for a female volunteer from the audience. With two swords, he would chop the woman in two, splattering blood all over while her horrified family cried and screamed. Then he'd rejoin the halves and spit water on them, and the young woman would be miraculously healed and whole once more. Not everybody appreciates a good illusion, though. When one foreign magician performed in front of the emperor, seeming to disembowel himself, the emperor was so grossed out that he put an end to the performance and ordered his border guards to forbid any foreign magicians from entering the empire.

Pillow Maker

You might be an expert in porcelain, a wood carver, or a stone carver. You make pillows, but not the fluffy, feather-filled kind. In ancient China, people expect pillows to be hard as stone. They are little rectangular platforms with a dip in the middle for resting the neck. Some pillows are more than just plain boxes, though—they're works of art. You might paint lines of poetry on one of your pillows or carve it into the shape of a tiger. Pillows can give the sleeper special qualities or ward off evil. If your customer wants a baby boy, then you should make her a sleeping bear to rest on. If she's prone to headaches, you should carve a pillow out of rosewood. Just make sure that all your pillows are comfortably hard and solid.

Iron Worker

You and other iron workers are employed by the emperor. You get paid in food or money, and you make a comfortable living. You have a hot job, though, in one of the government-owned blast furnaces. To shape iron, you must first heat it to 1130 degrees Celsius (2066 degrees Fahrenheit), the temperature at which it will melt. You stir the melted metal until it loses its carbon and the cast iron becomes wrought iron, which is much stronger. (The word for what you do is *chao*, which means "stir fry.") You pour the melted iron into a cast made in whatever shape you want. You've also discovered that wrought iron and cast iron combined can make steel. Your products are used to manufacture many things, including weapons and armor. Your steel swords are strong and sharp, and making them is said to be the art of harmonizing the hard and the soft.

Lacquer Worker

You are an artisan of the highest skill. You know how to take an object and make it almost indestructible. You can coat a wooden bowl so that it won't rot for centuries, even at the bottom of a lake. Your secret is the sap of the lac tree, which grows in western, northwestern, and eastern China. The sap isn't sweet like maple syrup. Instead, you refine it so that when it dries it forms a hard finish on whatever it coats. You put lacquer on all kinds of beautiful, expensive things for the rich: cups, dishes, and the combs and hairpins that court ladies use. You coat wooden sheaths for swords and shields. (Warriors definitely want their shields to be as impenetrable as possible.) Your services are also popular with undertakers. Everyone who can afford it wants a coffin that won't rot in the ground like plain wooden ones do.

It takes a team to lacquer any single object. There are different people in charge of priming, gilding, painting, engraving, and polishing. All those involved sign their name on the object once the painstaking work is complete.

Jade Worker

You are an expert with the jade stone, which requires careful cutting with the sharpest of knives. You don't want to mess up because jade is precious, like gold. Many of the things you make will be used in the imperial palace. Jade is believed to have magical qualities of preservation and to offer protection against evil spirits. It makes sense, then, that sometimes princes and other super-rich men are buried in jade suits. The suits don't end at the neck; they completely cover the corpse and are fitted around the nose, ears, and feet. They are made up of thousands of jade plaques, which it's your job to painstakingly cut and sand. Once you have all the plaques cut and have drilled tiny holes along the edges, you sew them together with gold or silver thread. You're multitalented— few people can boast of being a stone cutter and a tailor at the same time. These suits take ages to build; you're looking at a decade before a jade suit is ready to hand to your customer. Happily, most of them are preordered before your clients kick the bucket.

Master Craftsman, Terra-cotta Warriors

Let me give you a hand.

THE TERRA-COTTA ARMY

Archeologists to this day are still excavating the pits where the fantastic terra-cotta army was buried. There are likely more than 8,000 soldiers, as well as 130 chariots drawn by 520 horses and 150 cavalry horses buried in the tomb. The soldiers hold weapons, around 10,000 working crossbows, swords, and spears. The weapons were so well made that most of them are still sharp to this day, 2,000 years after they were buried. In addition to soldiers, there are also figures of officials, acrobats, strong men, and musicians, too. (Hey, if you're going to command an army in the afterlife, you should provide some entertainment for your soldiers.)

Whatever the emperor does, he does with style. Take his grave site—he's been planning it since he was 13 years old. The first emperor of Qin wished to rule in the afterlife, and it's impossible to rule without an army.

You are one of the 85 master craftsmen on this project, and you'll be working to create an entire army (complete with horses, carriages, and supplies) out of clay. Each craftsman has 10 to 12 assistants who do the less skilled work, like mixing clay. You've created a kind of assembly line to make the separate body parts before putting them together. It will still take a lifetime to complete this project, since the face of each of the 8,000 soldiers has to be different. Each detail on every figure, from height, hair, and facial expression to the tread on the soles of the shoes, is perfect and unique. Even the horses are individuals. You are also in charge of painting the warriors in stunning bright colors. It might seem a shame that your life's work will be buried, but at least it's your sculptures and not you who will be accompanying the emperor into the afterlife.

Chapter 11

Merchants and Service Worker Jobs

As a merchant, you made a good living selling pots and pans, or needles, or animals, but you got no respect. People thought you were dishonorable because you didn't grow food or make the items you sold yourself. According to the emperor, you were below everyone else in society. For this reason, you faced a lot of discrimination. There were excellent highways you could have traveled to get to where the markets were, for example, but you were not allowed to use them. You had to walk beside the highway on narrow, foot-worn tracks while the officials took the wide earthen roads. Even if you were rich, you were not allowed to hold office, own land, or ride horses. You might have been ashamed of what you did, but your silk clothes, large home, rich friends, and educated children would have been some comfort. If you were a lowly service worker, doing your job well would have to have been its own reward.

MONEY ON A STRING

When China was unified under the Qin Dynasty, the government got rid of local currencies and created a standard national coin. The copper coin was round with a square hole in the middle. By 1073, the government's mint had produced an estimated six million strings of coins, which contained a thousand copper coins each. The first paper money was issued by the government in 1024. Later, due to inflation and dynasty changes, silver and copper became popular currencies once more.

Merchant Junk Sailor

You work on a massive wooden boat called a junk. Your boat is anything but junky, however. Blame that impression on the slipperiness of translation. Your ship is a sight to behold: a huge, multi-sailed vessel constructed from soft wood. The junk has such a large rudder that it can take three sailors to control it. Waterproof compartments inside the ship keep things in storage organized, but also slow down flooding and make it easier to isolate a leak if one springs up. A strong hull is crucial because you might encounter one of the many typhoons that spring up in the South China Sea.

As far as boats go, you're in a roomy one. Some junks can be up to 137 meters (450 feet) in length and carry hundreds of sailors. Junks are often used by merchants, who sail as far as Ceylon, Arabia, and East Africa, looking for great deals to bring back home. Sometimes, under imperial orders, they trade silk, lacquerware, and porcelain for goods like pearls, spices, and ivory. As a sailor, you travel to all sorts of exotic places and see amazing things. Just don't apply if you're prone to seasickness.

Proto Banker

Tea Merchant

You work in the market, keeping other people's money safe. Shoppers bring heavy coins on a string to buy things, and your rich customers find it hard to carry around all their money. (What a problem to have!) You charge a fee for taking custody of their gold, silver, and coins to protect them from theft. You then issue your customers a check for the amount their valuables are worth. These checks are the first recorded usage of paper money. You're physically tough and always ready for a fight—you can't allow anyone to steal from you.

Although people first thought of tea as a medicinal drink, it soon took hold as a tasty all-weather beverage. Monks are especially fond of the drink because it helps them keep their eyes open during long meditations. You have a commodity that's easy to sell. It's light to carry, and just about everyone wants some. Leaves are plucked from the tea tree (*Camellia sinensis*) in spring. Workers then steam, pound, pat, and oven-roast them. They pack the final product in paper bags, which are wrapped in bamboo leaves or tree bark for shipping. You sell tea to customers at the market and to tea houses.

The rich take their tea seriously. Experts create lists of the best kinds of water to use (*Is this oolong best suited to spring water or glacial runoff?*) and 16 different ways to boil it, as well as the 24 utensils required to prepare and serve tea. Imagine all the washing up!

Noodle Maker

Restaurant Worker

You work at a popular noodle shop in the city. Your shop opens early in the morning and closes late at night, and it's busy, busy, busy. You make your noodles from flour, water, and sometimes eggs. You're very skilled. You take a lump of dough and pull it, then bounce it on your bamboo board. You stretch out the dough, fold it in half, and then start all over again. Soon you'll have pulled, bounced, and folded the dough into dozens of fine strands, all around the same thickness and ready to be dropped into boiling water. It's hard work, but you're fit, and your arms have become very muscular from your noodle exercise regime.

People eat your long and delicious noodles every day, but particularly on special occasions. They couldn't care less about a birthday cake, but birthday noodles are a must. During the New Year and on their birthday, your customers slurp up your noodles without biting down on them. Long noodles represent long life, and you wouldn't want to cut off your chances. That wouldn't be using your noodle!

You work at a local restaurant, serving the many hungry customers and travelers who are passing through. There are so many dishes that your customers have to consult your written menu to decide what to order. Your restaurant might specialize in serving only cold food, or hot or just-warm food. You don't have beef on the menu (after all, the bull is an important farm animal, doing much of the hard labor) or milk (yuck—only barbarians would drink the milk of a cow or goat). Along with any number of soups and noodle dishes, you offer favorites like fried tripe, steamed pancakes, mutton, and goose. You'd better have a good memory— a large dinner party might order 20 or more dishes. If you get one item wrong and a diner complains, you could get yelled at, have your salary docked, or even be kicked out of the restaurant for good.

Pearl Maker

Slave Merchant

Rich ladies love their jewelry. But you won't find many diamonds, rubies, or emeralds in their earrings, necklaces, rings, and bracelets. Diamonds are simply useful stones for tasks like grinding. Pearls are what a lady likes to wear. Jade and kingfisher feathers are also in high demand for those who value fashion. The wings of an emerald-green beetle might be used as a broach to attract men. Pearls are hard to find, however, which just makes everyone want them more. Your job is to create artificial pearls by boiling the nacre (the shiny inside of a seashell) in vinegar and then pulling it off in threads. You roll the nacre threads into spheres to look like pearls and poke a hole in them with a pig's bristle. That way you'll be able to string them into a necklace. You're not ready for that stage yet, though. You still need to put the spheres into the belly of a carp and steam the fish until it's overdone. Finally, you boil the "pearls" overnight in goat's milk—milk that you've already boiled and purified a couple of times—and then rinse them in the morning. Voilà! Fake pearls.

You don't deal *with* people, you deal *in* people. When poor farmers and peasants can no longer afford to feed their children, they come to you. Sometimes grown men will also allow themselves to be sold into slavery rather than starve to death. You have a large population to draw from. Times of famine are big business for you since even the government encourages parents to give up their children to the slave trade when the going gets tough.

Sometimes the people you trade are victims of kidnapping. Once they're yours, though, you won't let them go without turning a profit. You hate it when the government issues an edict freeing all slaves every now and again. That's terrible for business.

You treat your slaves like livestock. You keep men, women, and children in animal pens, and your slaves are sold at markets. If you're trying to sell to really rich people, you'll sometimes dress your slaves in gorgeous silk robes to show off their quality and good breeding. Wouldn't you think the cages would ruin the effect?

Chapter 12

Illegal Jobs

Every society has a criminal element, and imperial China was no different. Illegal jobs weren't necessarily immoral; they just didn't fall within the law. Revolutionary leaders and redressers of wrongs could have gotten into trouble for what they did, but they were driven by a sense of moral justice. Others, like assassins and pirates, sought money, infamy, and power. Beggars and vagabonds were forced into a life of illegal activities because they were too poor and powerless to live any other way. What about you? Are you stealing grain for your starving family, or pillaging a village for more gold?

Pirate Admiral

Assassin

You've got your sea legs, don't you? Good. You'll also need to be a great strategist, a business-person, and a superior intellect. The most famous pirate in all of China, Shi Xianggu, ended up commanding more ships than most governments have in their navy. In fact, she had more ships than all of China's navy, which made her impossible to catch. As a pirate admiral, you spend your days plotting attacks and branching out into other lucrative pursuits, like protection schemes, blackmail, and extortion. You live in tight quarters with a lot of rough men, and you need to make sure they understand you're the one leading them. At your command, your men will behead anyone who doesn't follow your orders and chop off the ears of anyone foolish enough to be a deserter.

As for retirement, you'll definitely want to negotiate a sweet deal like Shi Xianggu did. She terrorized everyone for decades, then accepted the government's offer to retire under total amnesty with all her loot. Life is good for a successful pirate.

You work for a group of powerful merchants. In fact, your bosses are so powerful they can flout all the rules they like. They dress like officials, which is strictly forbidden, and they have enough servants to make them seem like kings. They have influence in the courts as well. When one of your bosses breaks the law, or you do, no one is going to get punished—a wink and a nod will take care of it. As an assassin, you're the one doling out punishment to anyone who might have crossed your employers. You're ready to die for your bosses, and you'll kill anyone they ask you to without question. Your rich bosses are the law, and you're their enforcer.

Rebel Leader

Redresser of Wrongs

You don't really have a job—you have a calling. You take it upon yourself to help the poor, the humble, the disadvantaged. You likely have a fair bit of money, but you spend it on those in need. Basically, you're Batman without the costume and gadgets. The Chinese words that make up your title, *Jen* and *hsia*, are translated as "by resort to strength" and "to assist." You're not afraid of a fight, and you feel justified in using force to bring about what you believe is right. The law doesn't approve of what you do, but you're seen as an avenging hero by the people you protect. You keep a fair number of guests, or *shike*, at your house as a small private army so that the law won't bother you while you redress the wrongs in your community.

Have you had enough? Are you tired of seeing peasants overtaxed, overworked, and overburdened with corvée labor? Then rise up and organize the people against the corrupt government. To be a rebel leader, you'll need to be persuasive and passionate. You could be like Lu Mu, or "Mother Lu," as she was known to her friends and supporters. When her son was beheaded by the government for not punishing peasants who couldn't pay their taxes, Mother Lu sold her lands and opened a tavern to attract young men who would fight for her cause. She stockpiled weapons and started buying up horses. You too can lead a guerrilla war on sea and on land, gathering more than 10,000 supporters to kick out the government. Long live the rebel army!

Fake Buddhist Monk

You may not believe in Buddhism, but you do believe in conserving your time and making money. Monks and nuns are exempt from both taxes and conscription into the army and labor camps. It's easy to understand why you don't want to spend two to four years of your life digging graves or making bricks for the Great Wall. On the other hand, as a monk, you wouldn't be able to marry, eat meat, or drink alcohol. You know some savvy and less than ethical land-lords who have become bogus monks by getting ordination certificates (otherwise known as free passes) and then going back to their old lives with their wives and families. Sounds like a pretty neat solution, doesn't it? It might even be worth the risk of returning as a fruit fly in your next life.

Robber/Beggar/ Vagabond

You've had a rough go of it so far. You probably started as a farmer and then had a bad year. Due to drought, flooding, or a hard winter (pick one or all three), you had to sell your iron tools and oxen in order to pay taxes. The next year you borrowed money from a neighboring rich land owner to buy seed, and you exhausted yourself plowing the land by hand with wooden tools that broke easily. After another bad year (too hot, too cold, too dry, too wet), your kids were sold into slavery and the tiny bit of land you had was gone. Next, you worked in near-starving conditions for a land owner who treated you poorly. Now you live in the wilds, trying to rob and beg your way into getting enough food and clothing. It's no wonder rebel leaders look for people like you to join their ranks against kings and emperors. You're not afraid to fight because you've got nothing left to lose.

How about donating a little chicken soup to a dutiful monk?

Wait a minute... real monks don't eat meat!

RECOMMENDED FURTHER READING

Hume, Lotta Carswell. *Favorite Children's Stories from China and Tibet* (1962).

This charmingly illustrated book is great for anyone who loves fairy tales and who wants a taste of Chinese culture.

Kramer, Lance. *Great Ancient China Projects You Can Build Yourself* (2008).

If you've ever found history boring, you won't with this innovative and fun book. Comprehensive and informative, this book is as hands-on as it gets! If you've ever wanted to try out some of the neat things invented or used in ancient China, this book will help you do it. From making your own ink, noodles, or seismograph to designing a house with proper feng shui, this book has it all.

Loewe, Michael. *Everyday Life in Early Imperial China* (1968).

This book gives a comprehensive look at the Han dynasty in ancient China. Covering everything from peasants to civil servants, *Everyday Life in Early Imperial China* provides a broad overview of historical and geographical context and includes information on many aspects of society including the army, literature, city life, and technology of times. This is a wonderful book for those who want to dig a little deeper into the interesting and vibrant time of the Han Dynasty.

Patent, Dorothy Hinshaw. *The Incredible Story of China's Buried Warriors* (2000).

Filled with large color photos of the excavated warriors, *The Incredible Story of China's Buried Warriors* is perfect for those who want to know about how this incredible terra-cotta army was made. The book also gives some historical background of the times when the army was constructed.

Schomp, Virginia. *The Ancient Chinese* (2004).

This colorful book provides illustrations, art, and photos as well as timelines and examples of both historical events and day-to-day living. For a small book it is a thorough and concise introduction to the people who once lived in ancient China. This was one of the first books I used in my research, and it provides a very interesting and easy-to-read look at ancient China.

ACKNOWLEDGMENTS

The work of many authors has made this book possible. In particular, I would like to acknowledge Michael Loewe, Charles Ben, Barbara Bennett Peterso, Livia Kohn, Jane Shuter, Alan M. Klide, and Shiu H. Kung. A very special thank-you to editor Barbara Pulling, whose expertise and skill were much appreciated. Any errors are mine alone. Thanks and admiration to illustrator Martha Newbigging, whose eye for detail and humor are unfailing. My gratitude to designer Sheryl Shapiro, managing editor Katie Hearn, Tara Tovell, Colleen Ste. Marie, and the rest of the team at Annick Press for your wonderful work. Many thanks to the ever patient and always helpful children's librarians at Kingston Frontenac Public Library, Central Branch. As always, thanks to Tim McIntyre, my husband and editor. All of these people mentioned would have been smart enough to pass an ancient Chinese Civil Service exam.

INDEX

acrobats, 74, 75, 84
acupuncture, 49, 51–52, 54
acupuncturist, 51
administrator,
    county, 34
    grand, 7, 27, 34
alchemist, 41
ancestor worship, 8, 15, 19, 44, 50, 63
assassin, 90–91
astrologist, 40
astronomer, 40, 45

barbarians, 6, 62, 80, 88
beggar, 90, 93
bone diviner. *See* royal oracle
bronze, 8, 76, 81
    worker, 81
Buddhism, 9–10, 15, 17, 23, 43–44
    fake monks, 93
    monks, nuns, 47
    warrior monks, 48

calligrapher, 79
calligraphy, 38, 78–79
civil service, 10, 13, 16, 27, 32, 34, 38, 56
    exams, 13, 32, 37
commanderies, 7, 34, 38,
concubines, 19–20, 22–23, 25–26, 28, 30,
    39, 53
Confucianism, 9, 15, 38, 43–44, 56
    Confucius, 14–15
consort families, 30
convicts, 56, 68
corvée labor, 68–70, 92
court architect, 25

doctor, 11, 13, 25, 46, 49–52, 59
dynasties, 8, 18–19, 39, 44, 80
    Han, 10, 14, 20, 38
    Qin, 10, 85
    Shang, 8, 12
    Song, 38
    Sui, 10
    Tang, 7, 9, 18, 31, 38, 44, 53–54, 61, 79
    Zhou, 9, 12

education, 13, 26, 31, 38–39
    grand tutor to heir apparent, 21
    medical professor, 51
    private teacher, 38
    student, 38
embroidery, 31
emperor, 6–7, 9–12, 18–20, 22–30, 33–35,
    39–47, 53, 56, 58, 68, 70–72, 75,
    81–82, 84–85, 93
    child, 21
empress, 10, 14, 20–23, 26–27, 30, 39, 44,
    75, 79
    empress dowager, 20
    sacred and divine empress regnant, 23
    Teng, Empress Dowager, 20
    Zetian, Wu, 23
    Zhao, Wu, 9
endless chain, 65
    worker, 65
entertainers 19, 72–73
    dancers, singers, 30, 50
    opera actor, 74
eunuchs, 10, 26
exorcism, 50

fisherman, cormorants, 66

games, 28
geography, 6 –7
geomancer, 42
gods, 12, 19, 46, 63
gold bird guard, 59
grand administrators, 7, 27
grave digger, 70
Great Wall, 62, 68
    building, 69
    watchtower guard, 62
guest, 29

heir apparent. *See* emperor: child
historian, 39
    Qian, Sima, 39
horses, 28, 33

illusionist, 81
imperial chancellor, 33
imperial consort, 22
ink stick maker, 80
inventions, 6, 17, 42
    air conditioning, 18
    forensic entomology, 58
    gun powder, 42
    magnetic compass, 42
    paper, 42
    printing, 42
    seismograph, 42
inventor, 42
iron, 68, 76, 82, 93
    worker, 82

jade, 8, 29, 83, 89
    worker, 83
judge, 34, 58. *See also* magistrate
junk, 86

kings, 7, 9, 22, 27–28, 30, 61

lacquer, 11, 83, 86
    worker, 83
litter attendant, 71

magistrate, 34, 57–58
mail carrier, 36
mandate of heaven, 9, 12, 19
market, 59, 73, 75, 81, 85, 87, 89
    commandant, 59
master craftsman, terra-cotta warriors, 84
matchmaker, 49, 55
medicine, 9, 50, 51, 54, 59, 80
merchant, 11–13, 37, 44, 50, 59, 73, 75,
    85–91
    sailor, 86
    tea, 87
meritocracy, 13
midwife, 52
military, 10, 33–34, 36, 43, 56, 60–62
    conscripted, 60
    female warrior, 61
    watchtower guard, 62

minister
    coachman, 33
    herald, 24
    of ceremonies, 45
    of finance, 35
    of household, 23
    of justice, 58
    of the guards, 24
    of the imperial clan, 35
    steward, 25
money, 10, 13, 25, 29, 33, 44, 47, 63, 65,
    67, 72, 74, 81–82, 85, 87, 90, 92–93
musician, 7, 75, 84

night soil spreader, 66
nobles, 11, 13, 24, 27–28, 35, 37, 48, 53, 75
    women, 31
noodles, 88
    noodle maker, 88

painter, 79–80, 83
paper, 6, 10, 17, 42, 48, 76–77, 80, 85, 87,
    maker, 77
passports, 24
pearls, 29, 31, 80, 86, 89
    maker, 89
peasants, 7–9, 11–13, 23, 26, 28, 37, 47, 60,
    63, 68–69, 72–73, 75, 89, 92
    children, 37, 64
    female, 64
    male, 65
Pekingese caretaker, 26
Pekingese dogs, 26
period of disunity, 10
philosopher, 13, 15, 43
physiognomist, 53
pillow maker, 82
pirate admiral, 91
pirates, 14, 90–91
poet, 78
poetry, 14, 29, 39, 78, 82
population, 7
prefect, 24, 58
prefectures, 7, 34
priest, 46, 54, 81
princess, 29, 35, 61, 79
printer, 76
proto banker, 87

qi, 42, 51, 53, 78

rank, 11–13, 18, 20, 22, 24, 26–28, 30,
    32–34, 38, 56, 73,
rebel leader, 92
rebellion, 10, 12, 14, 61, 92–93
redresser of wrongs, 90, 92
restaurant worker, 88
robber. *See* beggar
royal oracle, 8, 45

salt, 10, 35, 68, 70
salt mine worker, 70
silk, 6, 17, 25–26, 31, 38, 79, 80, 85–86, 89
    maker, 67
Silk Road, 6
slaves, 52, 61, 65, 68, 71
    children, 72
    dark green head, 72
    government slave, 72
    merchant, 89
sorceress, 46

Taoism, 8, 14–15, 43–44
terra-cotta warriors, 84
thieves, 26, 29
trade, 6

vagabond. *See* beggar
veterinarians, 54

wailer, 54
warring states period, 8, 43
wet nurse, 53, 72
women, 14
    doctors, 50
    midwife, 52
    peasants, 64
    pirate, 91
    rebel, 92
    scholars, 39
    wailer, 54
    warrior, 61
    wet nurse, 53, 72

yin and yang, 40–41, 50–51, 54